The War on Terror

The War on Terror

The War on Terror

Reordering the World

NINAN KOSHY

LeftWord

First published in India in May 2003 by
LeftWord Books
12 Rajendra Prasad Road
New Delhi 110001
India
Phone: (91-11) 2335 9456, 2335 6966
Email: leftword@vsnl.com

LeftWord Books is a division of
Naya Rasta Publishers Pvt. Ltd.
27–29 Bhai Vir Singh Marg
New Delhi 110001
India

ISBN 81-87496-32-0

Printed at Progressive Printers
A 21 Jhilmil Industrial Area
Grand Trunk Road
Shahdara
Delhi 110 095
India

Contents

Preface

The first edition of this book was published by DAGA (Documentation for Action Groups in Asia), Hong Kong, in September 2002, one year after the terrorist attacks in New York and Washington. The book is an analysis of the projects and doctrines of the War on Terror declared by the President of the United States in response to the events of September 11, 2001. One country which fully endorsed the positions of the US was the UK. Tony Blair, the Prime Minister of Great Britain emerged as the most articulate supporter of President Bush's views. In fact, one of his celebrated speeches provided a framework for the analysis. Addressing the Labour Party Conference on October 2, 2001, just a few days before the Anglo-American invasion of Afghanistan, he said, 'the war against terrorists should be a far wider struggle for a new world order'. Linking this statement to Blair's own earlier remarks about the role of the US military in the global economic order and the theoretical formulations of some his top advisers on imperialism, the analysis deals with the relationship between the War on Terror and globalization, as well as the imperial features of the projected new world order.

It becomes thus clear that the War on Terror is an imperialist war to make the world secure for the global economic and strategic interests of the United States.

The analysis is made largely from an Asian perspective

taking into account that the main theatre of the War on Terror is Asia. The whole of Asia from West Asia to North East Asia has become the theatre of the war. It started in Central Asia with immediate consequences for South Asia. Already in January 2002, President Bush included North Korea in the 'axis of evil'. Soon after, the 'second front' was officially opened in the Philippines in South East Asia. As I mentioned in the Preface to the first edition, 'In West Asia, also called the Middle East, the ongoing wars against Palestine and Iraq were intensified and declared to be part of the War on Terror'. March 20, 2003 marked the US 'strike on Iraq' for occupation.

This edition published by LeftWord Books has been updated with developments that have occurred in the last eight months including the US invasion of Iraq. These developments, despite their breath-taking pace, have only confirmed the analysis and validated the interpretation already made in the first edition.

The War on Terror is reordering the world. A careful analysis of the events since September 11, 2001, will provide us useful insights to understand the shape of the new order that is emerging. The book is a modest attempt in this direction.

I am grateful to LeftWord Books for publishing this book at a time when the War on Terror has entered a new and critical stage.

April 11, 2003 Ninan Koshy

1

Introduction

The War on Terror was declared by George W. Bush, President of the United States of America, in response to the horrific events of September 11, 2001. More than an year and a half later, the war goes on unabated, with shifting aims, new targets, expanding scope and refurbished strategies.

The first declaration of war by the President was made on September 20 before a joint session of the US Congress. He identified Al Qaeda as the perpetrators of the attacks in New York and Washington on September 11 and accused Afghanistan of harbouring Al Qaeda leaders, particularly Osama bin Laden. He said that the leadership of Al Qaeda had great influence in controlling most of that country. 'In Afghanistan we see Al Qaeda's vision for the world'. He made demands on the Taliban 'to deliver to the US authorities all the leaders of Al Qaeda who hide in your land', 'close immediately and permanently every terrorist training camp in Afghanistan and hand over every terrorist and every person in their support structure'. By making it clear that these demands were not open to negotiations or discussions, the President was virtually giving an ultimatum to the rulers of Afghanistan.

In its early days, this was dubbed 'America's New War' by the CNN. The war was to be global in scope and for an indefinite period. 'Our war on terror begins with Al Qaeda but it does not end there. It will not end until every terrorist group of global reach has been found, stopped and defeated'. Further, 'Americans should not expect one battle, but a lengthy campaign unlike any other we have seen'.

The President addressed all nations of the world and outlined the choice before them. 'Every nation in every region now has a decision to make. Either you are with us or you are with the terrorists'. The reason proffered was that 'This is not just America's fight alone. What is at stake is not just America's freedom. This is the world's fight. This is civilization's fight'. The attack may have taken place on American soil, but the whole world had to be mobilized because it was an attack on freedom and civilization in the whole world. Any nation not joining the war on America's side was supporting terrorists. This was hardly a choice; it was a command which brooked no disobedience. The President of the mightiest nation on earth was laying down the law for the whole world.

But who was the war to be against? What was to be the nature of the war? The President had no intention of making such things clear. The agenda was left completely open-ended, to be added to, changed, amended, revised as he pleased. The rest of the world would be told bits and pieces about it as and when the US establishment saw fit. As Stanley Hoffman wrote,

> The first question that came to any one's mind has still not been answered. Whom are we fighting? If it is bin Laden and his associates, formidable as they may be, we risk finding that dismantling their network is likely to be a slow and penetrating task in a world without walls and even successes in this particular struggle will not put an end to many other murderous forms of terrorism. . . . To proclaim a war on terrorism in general, even if one means only terrorist cells and forces not directly sponsored by states, is ambitious indeed, for we need to distinguish among

> types of terrorists. . . . A determined project of ridding the world of all rogues and terrorists is a dream that would be seen abroad as a demonstration of rabid imperialism.[1]

On the other side of the Atlantic, British Prime Minister Tony Blair, who emerged as the most eloquent champion of the War on Terror, was more specific about the target. 'Any action taken will be against the terrorist network of bin Laden. . . . As for the Taliban, they can surrender the terrorists or face the consequences'. He was also more visionary about its aims. For him, the fight was not only for freedom but also for justice for the wretched of the earth. 'The starving, the wretched, the dispossessed, the ignorant, those living in squalor from the deserts of North Africa to the slums of Gaza, to the mountain ranges of Afghanistan, they too are our cause'.[2]

The second declaration of war came from President Bush as part of his State of the Union address on January 29, 2002. By that time Taliban had been ousted from power in Afghanistan and a new regime installed. President Bush said, 'What we have found in Afghanistan confirms that far from ending there our war against terror is only beginning'. He should have actually said, 'what we have *not* found in Afghanistan', for the Americans did not find Osama bin Laden, whom the President had pledged to find 'alive or dead'. One of the important declared aims of the War on Terror was 'to bring Osama bin Laden to justice or bring justice to him'.

President Bush said that the US would continue to be 'steadfast, patient and persistent in the pursuit of two great objectives'. 'First we shall shut down terrorist camps, disrupt terrorist plans and bring terrorists to justice'. This was of course a reiteration of an objective in the first declaration itself. The second objective, however, had nothing to do with responding to the

September 11 attacks but related to an entirely different kind of terror. 'We must prevent the terrorists and regimes who seek chemical, biological and nuclear weapons from threatening the US and the world'. The ambit was widening and the scope was expanding. New enemies were being listed; new targets were being identified. The War on Terror, he said, will now turn to 'regimes that sponsor terror from threatening America or our friends and allies with weapons of mass destruction'. He named North Korea, Iran and Iraq and said, 'States like these and their terrorist allies constitute an axis of evil aiming to threaten the peace of the world'. Bush gave a clear warning to 'the axis of evil'.

In the same speech Bush referred to another kind of expansion of the War on Terror. It was expanding geographically and new fronts were being opened. 'While the most visible military action is in Afghanistan, America is acting elsewhere. We now have troops in Philippines. Our soldiers are working with the Bosnian government. Our navy is patrolling the coast of Africa'. Bush was claiming that the War on Terror was not only in Central Asia but extended to South East Asia and to parts of Africa too. By declaring war against the 'axis of evil' he was giving notice of extending the war to the Middle East (West Asia) and North East Asia. The whole Asian region from West Asia to North East Asia, through Central, South and South East Asia was declared as the theatre of America's War on Terror.

Naturally, the term 'axis of evil' caused a lot of confusion and controversy. Axis is the relation between countries, regarded as a common pivot on which they revolve. 'The Axis' was the political association of 1936, between Italy and Germany and later Japan, which became also a military alliance during the Second World War. It was far from clear what the common pivot in Bush's 'axis of evil' was. There is practically no relation among the three countries named by Bush. In fact, these three countries hardly constitute an organized alliance against the US and there is no valid comparison with the Axis of the Second World War. Iran and Iraq are at loggerheads, and despite North Korea reportedly harbouring a few members of the Japanese Red Army, it has not sponsored any terrorist attacks for a long time.

President Bush implicitly threatened to expand the war on terrorism to countries that are developing weapons of mass destruction. Although such rhetoric may be sabre rattling to intimidate those nations, the possibility of an expansion of the war is a real and dangerous possibility. This begs the question: although North Korea, Iran and Iraq may be developing or have acquired weapons of mass destruction, so have many other nations. According to the Pentagon, 12 nations have nuclear weapon programmes, 13 have biological weapons, 16 have chemical weapons and 18 have ballistic missiles. 'Is the US President prepared to attack all of these nations?' asks Ivan Eland of the Cato Institute.[3]

The fact is that the US must live with an increasing number of nations, including its allies, that have acquired weapons of mass destruction. North Korea, Iran and Iraq are nations on the other side of the world from the US and ought not to be natural enemies of the US – unless the US keeps intervening in their regions. Furthermore, by threatening to attack North Korea, Iran or Iraq, the US could exacerbate the proliferation problem rather than reduce it. Other nations might believe they could be next and think that working on missiles and weapons of mass destruction is the only way to keep out a superpower bent on militarily intervening everywhere in the name of fighting terrorism.

A perpetual state of war – in Bush's words, 'a lengthy campaign unlike any other we have seen' – can undermine economic recovery, does not comport with the values that America claims to uphold, and will likely lead to the erosion of constitutional liberties and the accumulation of too much power in the executive branch not only in the US but also in many countries that support the War on Terror. A seemingly unprovoked war against another Muslim country – either Iran or Iraq or both – will have repercussions all over the world including the spread of terrorism. Thus an expanded US war on terrorism could generate more terrorism, rather than prevent or reduce it.

Allies of the US were confused and felt the phrase 'axis of evil' was misleading. Bush's speech seemed to have frightened America's allies quite as much as it scared its enemies – 'evil' or otherwise. Secretary of State Colin Powell's laboured explanation that 'it does not mean that we are ready to invade any one or that we are not willing to engage in dialogue' was not convincing, especially because everybody knew that doors were suddenly opening in Washington, in the State Department and the Pentagon, for Iraqi opposition groups. An attack on Iraq, many thought, was imminent.

Bush took special pride in the enormous increase in the defence budget. 'My budget includes the largest increase in defence spending in two decades, because while the price of freedom and security is high, it is never too high. Whatever it costs to defend our country we will pay it', he said in his State of the Union address. Bush proposed a new budget of $379 billion, an increase of 48 billion over the already unexpectedly high 2001 budget, the *increase alone* being larger than any other nation's military budget. As one commentator put it, 'the War on Terror will involve more frequent military intervention with less of an attempt to placate internal sensibilities and with the constant excuse of protecting American security. It will involve more overt appeals to Western cultural supremacy, although couched in universalist and moralistic terms'.[4]

A number of European leaders indicated that they would

oppose military action against the states identified by President Bush as the 'axis of evil'. Senior European Union representatives made it clear that they 'do not agree with that kind of policy'. European Union's foreign policy chief Javier Solana urged the US to act multilaterally and not as a 'global unilateralist'. British Foreign Secretary Jack Straw thought that the 'axis of evil speech was more of a vote winning tactic in the forthcoming elections than a military strategy'.[5]

Disregarding everybody's discomfiture, the Bush administration appeared to revel in the phrase. In a speech on May 7, 2002, entitled 'Beyond the Axis of Evil', the US Under-Secretary of State John Bolton added Cuba, Libya and Syria to the list of nations that the US claims are deliberately seeking to obtain chemical or biological weapons. He said that these nations could be grouped with the 'axis of evil' states – Iraq, Iran and North Korea – in actively developing weapons of mass destruction. He also warned that the US would take action.[6] Bolton singled out Cuba for particular criticism and accused it of developing biological weapons and sharing its expertise with Washington's enemies. He presented no evidence for his claims, and pointed only to Cuba's advanced biomedical industry and Fidel Castro's visit the previous year to three 'rogue states' accused by the US of sponsoring terrorism: Iraq, Syria and Libya. A war front was being opened in Latin America. The administration also accused FARC rebels in Colombia of supporting anti-US terrorism, while calling for increased military aid to Bogota. Larry Birns, head of the Council on Hemispheric Affairs think tank in Washington, said, 'What is dangerous now is that the anti-terror war has no standards and criteria. It is whatever the Bush administration says is at any given moment'. Critics of the administration's policies in Latin America described the accusation as an attempt to exploit popular support for the War on Terror to pursue a rightwing political agenda.

President Bush's speech on June 4, 2002 to the graduating class of the US Military Academy at West Point, New York took the war to a new doctrinal plane. He claimed that the doctrines of deterrence and defence were not sufficient for the War on Terror:

> For much of the last century, America's defence relied on the Cold War doctrines of deterrence and containment. . . . Deterrence means nothing against shadowy terrorist networks with no nation or citizen to defend. Containment is not possible with unbalanced dictators when weapons of mass destruction can deliver these weapons on missiles or secretly provide them to terrorist allies. . . . We must take the battle to the enemy, disrupt his plans and confront the worst threats before they emerge. . . . The only path to safety is action. And this nation will act.

In other words, the War on Terror will not be a war on the defensive. This is called 'hot pre-emption' though Bush did not use the specific phrase. He was indicating a new strategic doctrine evolving in Washington in the context of the War on Terror. The moral high ground in the War on Terror, which the President had claimed from the very outset, was pushed to the front in the West Point address. 'Because the war on terror will require resolve and patience it will also require firm moral purpose. In this way our struggle is similar to the Cold War'.

The comparison of the War on Terror to the Cold War had been made in many Western circles soon after September 11. The War on Terror is the war against 'the evil of terror', as the Cold War was the war against the 'evil of communism', it was claimed. The United States was then, is now, and always will be on the side of good. If the Cold War took half a century, the War on Terror could take just as long.

The comparison involves a gross distortion of history, as

well as a falsification of the aims and methods that underlie the current military offensive of the United States. The Bush administration is promoting a myth about the Cold War to provide a new rationalization for pursuing the geopolitical and economic interests of American capitalism. At the same time, the US ruling elite hopes to utilize the spectre of global terrorism as a new external peril, supplanting the Soviet 'red' menace, in order to forge a political consensus behind its reactionary social agenda at home and abroad and militaristic foreign policy.

A *New York Times* column of October 6, 2002 had the title, 'The 40-Year War'. The commentary was written by Bill Keller, the newspaper's former Moscow correspondent, who is now one of its senior editors. Keller cited John Lewis Gaddis, the 'dean of Cold War studies'.

> Communism in the 1950s, Professor Gaddis points out, was seen not as a rival state but as a fearsome, state-sponsored conspiracy, one that threatened us from within as well as externally. The American response was 'containment', a kind of global gopher hunt aimed at countering Communist influence wherever it surfaced, using diplomacy and economic power and armed proxies more often than American military might. . . . Like the Cold War, this one, while it lasts, will assert a gravitational pull on everything. It will determine who our friends are, revise our priorities and test the elasticity of our ideals.

The three speeches of President Bush – to the Joint Session of the Congress, the State of the Union, and to the West Point graduates – have to be taken together to understand the different dimensions and implications of the War on Terror.

The first declaration of war was made soon after the tragic events of September 11. Only a preliminary list of enemies was announced then. As the war went on new names were added. Even after three declarations, the list is apparently not complete. Bush told the West Point graduates, 'You will lead a military that must be ready to strike at a moment's notice in any dark corner of the world'. The United States is ready to send its forces to any part of the world in its War on Terror.

The lack of clarity as to 'who are the enemies?' raises many questions. When will this War on Terror end? How will it end? If the enemy surrenders or the enemy is defeated the war will end. But in this war in which there is a continuous addition to the list of enemies as the war advances, and the enemies are terrorists all over the world, and the US military is 'ready to strike at a moment's notice in any dark corner of the world' how will one determine the defeat of the enemy or the victory of the US? Although it was claimed that the War on Terror is different from other wars, and that it will be fought on many levels and in many forms, it actually began in the most conventional way with an attack on a hapless country. There are disturbing ethical issues involved in the manner in which enemies are portrayed and identified and the means by which the War on Terror is waged.

Daniel Werner takes up this question in the *New York Times*:

> Concern with future attacks is being presented as open-ended in time and place. There is no longer a clear necessity to link an enemy to specific events or to say when the war can be declared over. If in the future, one person gets on with explosives in his shoes, is the war against terror still on? It is difficult to imagine the limits of the war and to see how the heightened sense of national security could be diminished. The United States appears to be entering a situation of hypersensitivity wherein any threat to its national security justifies enormous sacrifices of resources and eventually civil liberties.[7]

In the weeks following the September 11 terrorist attacks Bush administration officials frequently declared, 'everything has changed' without specifying precisely how. Certainly for modern America, the attack was singular in its audacity and magnitude. And it aroused uniquely strong and persistent support among Americans for vigorous military action abroad. But neither the terrorist threat nor the conditions that shaped it were new; September 11 had been gestating for some time. The declarations of change are best understood as the announcement of a new spirit in US security policy – not a New World, but a new thrust in America's approach to the world. The declarations of War on Terror showed that given the strategic power and reach of the United States, this new spirit would touch all the world's shores and borders. In this sense, the statement 'everything has changed' was not so much an observation on what had happened but a promise that everything *will* change. Needless to say, this promise tantamounts to a threat.

In the first few days after September 11, the US media, notably CNN, called it 'America's New War'. Uncomfortable questions about America's 'old wars' and the unilateralist tone of the slogan soon led to it being substituted with 'war on terrorism' or, for rhyme if not for reason, 'war on terror'. The term, however, still needed to be explained. Raphael Perl, a specialist in international affairs with the Congressional Research Service, in a speech before the German Council on Foreign Relations, Berlin, Germany, on July 2, 2002, provided an explanation. Presumably, he felt that even Germans had not understood the term almost a year after it was coined with glitter in Washington.

> It is impossible to discuss United States' counter-terrorism policy in the wake of September 11 without use of the word 'war'. US leaders have repeatedly characterized recent terrorist actions

> and America's response to the tragedy and horror of September 11th as a global 'war'.
>
> Yet many, especially outside the United States, see the phrase 'War on Terrorism' as a misnomer. When members of the public think of war in the traditional sense, one generally thinks of nations fighting nations. When military tacticians think of war, they tend to think in terms of superior military firepower to be used against enemies who are clearly identified. Legal scholars, when they think of war, tend to think in terms of universally accepted rules of conduct or constraints. Traditionally wars end in a decisive victory or negotiated peace. But the war on terrorism defies many, if not all these notions. Most of all it is not likely to have a decisive end. On the international diplomatic front, the global war on terrorism is more akin to an initiative – an ongoing process of indefinite duration. Wars are won or lost, but initiatives are measured in degrees of success as the years pass. That is what we will face for the foreseeable future: measured success, not victory.[8]

The US begins the 21st century in a position of world strength that rivals the great empires of the past – from ancient Rome to Victorian Britain. Its economy accounts for 22 per cent of world output, and it leads the world in all of the most cutting-edge technologies. Its military spends more than the 25 next largest militaries in the world. And the combined spending of the US and its most loyal allies – the NATO countries, South Korea and Japan – outdistances military spending in the rest of the world.

Daniel Werner holds the view that 'the United States appears at this time to be marching into a situation that fits [Paul] Kennedy's description of imperial decline'. In 1987, the Yale University historian Paul Kennedy described the rise and fall of empires. He analysed how all imperial powers arrived at a point of overreach that eventually destroyed the empire. Too much concern for security and disproportionate spending on defence were endemic to the fall of all previous empires he studied. Kennedy's book set off an important reaction in the United States in the late 1980s. It laid out the consequences of the superpower contest with the Soviet Union in terms of mutual imperial over stretches instead of mutual assured destruction. Werner remarks, 'What is so intriguing about the war on terrorism is that following the implosion of the Soviet Union due to its imperial overreach the United States seems to be embarking on a war that may have similar effects'.[9]

The War on Terror succeeded the Cold War. The peace dividend from the end of confrontation with the Soviet Union did not materialize. New enemies were found or invented: 'rogue states', 'states of concern' and now with the War on Terror, 'the axis of evil'. While the war against communism was international, it was focused. The War on Terror is global and diffused. Anyone who is not with the US in this war is with the terrorists. The US paints the world in black and white, with no shades of grey in between. Yet, the US is probably both incapable of securing that form of domination and unwilling to understand its implications. The open-ended war against potential enemies is highly dangerous and a continuing threat to peace.

The US has developed a fine art of producing justifications for public consumption for all US military operations. George Bush (Sr.) cast the 1991 Gulf War for oil as a noble effort to show that 'naked aggression would not stand' and for a 'New World order'. In 1999, what was actually a war to preserve NATO's 'credibility' was sold to the public as a humanitarian operation to save Kosovar refugees. The current George Bush's War on Terror is no different. If Bush was simply interested in 'bringing to justice' the perpetrators of the September 11 attacks, he wouldn't be launching an unending, open-ended War on Terror. Bush's constant talk of 'defending freedom' and vanquishing 'evildoers' deliberately obscures the geopolitical and imperial aims of the US in this war.

Strobe Talbott, who was President Clinton's special envoy during the Kosovo War explained, 'The American people have never accepted traditional geopolitics or pure balance of power calculations as sufficient reason to expend national treasure or to dispatch American soldiers to foreign lands. Throughout this [twentieth] century, the US government has explained its decisions to send troops "over there" with some invocation of democracy and its defence'.[10] The War on Terror follows this tradition.

Notes

1. Stanley Hoffman, *The New York Review of Books*, November 1, 2001.
2. Tony Blair's Address to the Labour Party Conference, *The Guardian*, October 3, 2001.
3. Ivan Eland, Cato Institute, February 8, 2002, available at www.cato.org/dailys/02802html.
4. Rahul Mahajan, 'The State of the Union and the New Cold War', *Commondreams*, February 1, 2002.
5. *The Guardian*, February 4, 2002.
6. Daniel Werner, *New York Times*, May 8, 2002.
7. Ibid.
8. US Department of State, *International Information Programs*, July 2, 2002.
9. Daniel Werner, *New York Times*, May 8, 2002.
10. Quoted in Mark Curtis, *The Great Deception, Anglo-American Power and World Order*, London: Pluto Press, 1996, p. 40.

2

September Eleven

It was an ordinary day, a fine morning. People were engaged in their normal work in the World Trade Centre in New York and the Pentagon in Washington. That morning, a group of international terrorists converted passenger planes into precision guided missiles and crashed them into the buildings. If the passengers in a fourth plane had not resisted and sacrificed themselves, this plane would presumably have hit the Capitol Hill or the While House. The targets represented not only the power of America but also its ideology and policies that have affected the whole world. It was an awesome event and an entirely new experience for the United States. The world watched in shocked disbelief as one, and then the other tower of the WTC collapsed in a heap of rubble and mangled steel. September 11, 2001 will remain forever etched in the memory and history of America. It was the first time after the Second World War that the US was attacked on its own soil. The attacks, which destroyed the lives of some three thousand people, deserve to be condemned in the strongest terms. The pain and agony of tens of thousands of people waiting and searching for their loved ones should not be forgotten as one tries to understand the import of September 11.

The new technique of using a fuel-filled passenger plane as a powerful weapon of destruction, was not anticipated by the defence establishment of the US or any other nation. This was not in the calculations or threat perceptions of their experts. Fiction writers had imagined such scenarios, but no one thought it could become a fact. The strikes themselves were of course meticulously planned, clearly targeting the icons of America's military and economic power, and the drama of attracting maximum attention of the visual media was equally meticulously built into it.

Perceptions of terrorism changed on that day suddenly and completely. Some observers coined the term 'hyperterrorism' in the immediate aftermath of the strikes, as if to confirm that nothing would ever be the same again. A hitherto unimagined threshold had been crossed. The scale of the event surpassed all limits of credibility. The technique of attack of September 11 will doubtless be repeated somewhere under other circumstances. A new weapon has been fashioned and tested successfully. The history of warfare proves that when a weapon is used, no matter how horrific its effects, it will generate the fear that someone somewhere will use it again. This was the case with gas after 1918, and with the aerial bombing of cities post-Guernica 1937. This has also been the fear about nuclear weapons in the last fifty-seven years after Hiroshima.

The cruelty of the perpetrators of the crime was matched by the degree of sophistication in their technique and the selection of their targets. The terrorists managed an electronic coup. The images of the strikes and the resultant destruction were beamed live to television screens around the world and entered drawing rooms and public places within minutes of the first strike. The images were repeatedly flashed on television screens for weeks afterwards. No other event has ever achieved such mass media attention in such a sensational manner.

The world realized it was dealing with a new kind of terrorism, highly sophisticated, global in its reach, organization and objectives. Yet this was an act of terror with no specific demands; it was not as if the terrorists were demanding the independence of a country, or some concrete political concessions, or the installation of a particular regime, or the release of some political prisoners. The strikes were intended to convey a message. While there was no agreement on the specifics of the message, broadly it appeared to be a warning against the behaviour of the US in the world and the way it exercised power. It was a protest against the US; many thought it was a punishment.

It was not surprising that US intelligence agencies, notably the Federal Bureau of Investigation (FBI) and the Central Intelligence Agency (CIA), were criticized for their apparent failure. On the other side, it was claimed that while there were warnings of attacks against the US, they were rather general in nature and not specific enough to follow through with preventive action. Nearly all previous attacks against the US had been attacks outside the US, on US personnel, institutions, installations, airplanes or ships. The intelligence agencies acted on the assumption that the likelihood of an attack on US soil was low. The assumption was that the homeland was not vulnerable. They went wrong and the US had to pay a very high cost.

There were reports at that time that the Israeli intelligence had specific information about plans for terrorist attacks inside the US and that this information had been conveyed to the US intelligence agencies. However, the Israeli Foreign Minister Shimon Peres, in an interview to CNN, said Israel had only general information about possible attacks on the US and there was no specific information about targets or modes of attack.

More damagingly, around the middle of May 2002 reports circulated in Washington that President Bush had been briefed on the danger of a terrorist attack involving the hijacking of US airliners more than a month before September 11. Despite the warning, the reports said, that the White House took no action to forestall the deadliest terrorist action in US history or to warn the public. CBS news reported on May 15, 2002 that Bush had received a CIA briefing on August 6, 2001, five weeks before the attack on World Trade Centre, which suggested that an airplane hijacking linked to Osama bin Laden was an imminent possibility. Congressional circles took particular note of the coincidence of the August 6 briefing and two FBI reports, one from the Phoenix, Arizona office on July 10, the other from Minneapolis on August 13 which focused attention on suspicion that Al Qaeda operatives were using US flight schools and cited possible links to Osama bin Laden. The Minneapolis FBI agents reported the detention of Zaccarias Moussaoui, the French-Moroccan immigrant who wanted to learn how to fly a Boeing 747, but not take off or land. One e-mail from a Minneapolis FBI agent described Moussaoui as someone who might fly a jumbo jet into the World Trade Centre. Both reports were ignored by the FBI headquarters.

Several senators, Republican as well as Democrat, said the revelations about advance warnings raised the issue of whether the September 11 attacks could have been prevented, saving thousands of lives. John McCain, Arizona Republican and former candidate for the Republican presidential nomination, said, 'There were two separate FBI reports plus a CIA warning, none of which were co-ordinated. The question is, if all three had been connected, would that have led to more vigorous activity'. The explanations given by the administration have not been convincing to the general public.

There are many who view the attacks on September 11 as just punishment for US policies and actions and for the havoc they have caused in many parts of the world. This attitude is unethical for the reason that those who were actually punished, those who lost their lives in the attacks, were innocent and they came from many countries. But it cannot be denied that there is widespread anger against American policies and actions. Amongst many sections of the people around the world, justifiably or not, American actions have generated revulsion and hatred. To say that these were reflected in the attacks is not an attempt to justify or even explain the reasons for the terrorist actions.

The claim by President Bush that the attacks were perpetrated by those who were opposed to freedom and democracy in the United States and fighting against civilization was not found convincing even by many nations which joined the grand coalition in the War on Terror. As Moises Naim wrote,

> For all the post-September 11 focus on Islamic anti-Americanism, the world's reaction has in fact exposed the variety, complexity and ubiquity of antipathy towards the US. In Argentina, Hebe de Bonafini, an internationally known human rights activist and president of the association of the Mothers of Plaza de Mayo (mothers of Argentineans who disappeared during the dictatorships) has said, 'when the attack happened I felt happiness'. In France, the editor of *Le Monde Diplomatique* offered his summary of the world's reaction: 'What is happening to (Americans) is too bad but they had it coming'.[1]

Naim said that anti-Americanism's most frequent expressions usually reflect a mish-mash of grievances. 'But one can identify five types, politico-economic, historical, religious, cultural and psychological.'

> Politico-economic anti-Americanism represents a reaction to current US foreign policies, support for Israel or for repressive governments in the Middle East; the US's role in the Balkans; its embargo on Iraq and Cuba; the lack of support for the Kyoto

protocol on climate change or for the establishment of the international criminal court. US economic policies also draw fire, whether for limits of imports from poor countries or for the use of International Monetary Fund and the World Bank to advance US interests.[2]

Naim points out that historical anti-Americanism has its roots in past US behaviour. In a column entitled 'The Last September 11' Chilean novelist and dramatist Ariel Dorfman reminds his readers that it was on September 11, 1973 that the democratically elected government of Salvador Allende, the socialist president of Chile, was overthrown in a military coup backed by the US. 'Both in Chile in 1973 and in the States today, terror descended from the sky to destroy the symbols of national identity, the palace of the president in Chile, the icons of financial and military power in New York and Washington'. Many other countries can remember similar dates. Naim continues,

> Religious anti-Americanism is most violently expressed by Islamic fundamentalists. . . . But religious fundamentalism is by no means exclusively Muslim. Roman Catholic liberation theologians, Greek Orthodox prelates, fundamentalist Jewish rabbis and US tele-evangelists also condemn American society's 'corrupting immorality'. . . . Cultural anti-Americanism is stirred by the American way of life to influence and often displace local cultures. . . . Psychological anti-Americanism is fuelled by jealousy, resentment, ambivalence and crushed expectations.[3]

Naim highlights the fact that globalization provides a climate for anti-Americanism.

In the early 1990s, millions around the world believed that it

> was just a matter of time before economic liberalization, political reforms and globalization propelled their standard of living closer to that enjoyed by Americans. Ten years later, Americans are richer while people in most transition economies and emerging markets still struggle, their frustration heightened by cheap, almost universal access to images and information about how much better Americans live.[4]

We need to closely examine the notion of an anti-Americanism supposedly based on religion. There are many who describe the attacks of September 11 as 'Islamic terrorism'. There are those who argue the response should be a 'crusade'.

One book that has been a bestseller after September 11 is *The Clash of Civilizations* by Samuel P. Huntington. Huntington's thesis is claimed to be the authoritative interpretation of a dimension that is decisive and at the very centre of global politics. Huntington says:

> It is my hypothesis that the fundamental source of conflict in this New World will not be primarily ideological or primarily economic. The great divisions among humankind and the dominating source of conflict will be cultural. Nation states will remain the most powerful actors in world affairs, but the principal conflicts of global politics will occur between nations and groups of different civilizations. The clash of civilizations will dominate global politics. The fault lines between civilizations will be the battle lines of the future.[5]

In Huntington's view, then, all conflicts are religious, since civilizations are described as cultures and cultures are made synonymous with religions. In a provocative thesis, he claims that 'Contemporary global politics is the age of Muslim wars.

Muslims fight each other and fight non-Muslims far more than do peoples of other civilizations, Muslims wars have replaced the Cold War as the principal form of international conflict. These wars include wars of terrorism, guerrilla wars, civil wars and interstate conflicts.'[6] He further argues that the 'new war', as administration officials termed the violence that began September 11, is not so new.

> It is a continuation and escalation of previous patterns of violence involving Muslims. Earlier Muslim terrorism had, however, been sporadic and in comparison relatively limited. . . . Beginning in 1993 the principal attacks on Americans and American facilities all appear to have originated with Osama bin Laden. September 11 revealed the existence of his sizeable global terrorist network with cells in perhaps 40 countries and with the expertise and resources to attempt well-planned simultaneous attacks. Also for the first time, the network struck with devastating effects within the United States. . . . The Age of Muslim wars had come home to America.[7]

In reality, however, neither states nor civilizations are anything like as united and monolithic as Huntington's account logically requires. The current conflict pits members of the same civilization against one another in both the Muslim and non-Muslim worlds. In an article 'The Clash of Ignorance' Edward Said commented that Huntington does not have time

> to spare for the internal dynamics and plurality of every civilization, or for the fact that the major contest in most modern cultures concerns the definition or interpretation of each culture, or for the unattractive possibility that a great deal of demagogy and downright ignorance is involved in presuming to speak for

> a whole religion or civilization. No, the West is the West and Islam is Islam.
>
> The carefully planned and horrendous, pathologically motivated suicide attack and mass slaughter by a small group of deranged militants has been turned into proof of Huntington's theses. Instead of seeing it for what it is – the capture of big ideas (I use the word loosely) by a tiny band of crazed fanatics for criminal purposes – international luminaries from former Pakistani Prime Minister Benazir Bhutto to Italian Prime Minister Silvio Berlusconi have pontificated about Islam's troubles, and in the latter's case have used Huntington's ideas to rant on about the West's superiority.[8]

In a remarkable series of three articles published between January and March 1999 in *Dawn*, Pakistan's most respected weekly, the late Eqbal Ahmad, writing for a Muslim audience, analysed what he called the roots of the religious right, coming down very harshly on the mutilations of Islam by absolutists and fanatical tyrants whose obsession with regulating personal behaviour promotes 'an Islamic order reduced to a penal code, stripped of its humanism, aesthetics, intellectual quests, and spirited devotion'. And this 'entails an absolute assertion of one, generally de-contextualized aspect of religion and a total disregard of another. The phenomenon distorts religion, debases tradition, and twists the political process wherever it unfolds'. As a timely instance of this debasement, Ahmad proceeds first to present the rich, complex, pluralist meaning of the word *jihad* and then goes on to show that in the word's current confinement to indiscriminate war against presumed enemies, it is impossible 'to recognize the Islamic – religion, society, culture, history or politics – as lived and experienced by Muslims through the ages'. The modern Islamists, Ahmad concludes, are 'concerned with power, not with the soul; with the mobilization of people for political purposes rather than with sharing and alleviating their sufferings and aspirations. Theirs is a very limited and time-bound political agenda.' What has made matters worse is that similar distortions and zealotry occur in the 'Jewish' and 'Christian' universes of discourse.

A little elaboration may be useful about the economic causes of anti-Americanism. An *International Herald Tribune/PEW* poll suggested in December 2001 that much of the world views the attacks as a symptom of unusually bitter polarization between 'haves' and 'have-nots'. 'The danger for America is that its overwhelming power is feeding resentment – in the same countries that also feel they are missing out on the spoils of economic progress'. Marwan Bishara, an Israeli Arab commentator who teaches international relations at the American University in Paris sees 'an asymmetric threat from terrorists growing out of the incredible quantitative difference of force and of riches between North and South. . . . When people feel so inferior militarily and economically, they adopt asymmetric means – not the usual means – to activate what they want'.[9]

In a prescient article in *The Economist* back in April 2001, the British economist Robert Wade wrote of a threat posed by those whom economic globalization has left out. Wade was careful to point out that there was no direct causal connection between deprivation and terrorism and said that the link between the two should be seen in terms of probabilities.

> It is a matter of conditions providing the nurturing environment in which the ideas of terrorism for example take root. They can then be crystallized out by people like Osama bin Laden. They may not be crystallized out, they may not take the form of hitting at the US as distinct from hitting at their own rulers.

> . . . Poverty does not help though – nor does the fact that while the West has been trumpeting the virtues of globalization the gap between rich and poor has actually been widening. . . . Meanwhile, the US aid budget has been declining very substantially over the 80s and 90s. So the US is seen on the one hand as this great looming superpower, rigging the world system in its own interest and on the other hand it is doing very little by way of aid.[10]

It should not be forgotten that Islamic extremism has taken shape and grown stronger criticizing the support that the US gives to Israel in its policies against Palestinians. The point here is not whether those who launched the attacks against the US are genuinely interested in solving the Palestinian issue. They may be using the issue as a strategy. But that does not mean that the issue and the plight of the Palestinians can be ignored. American media and opinion makers have repeatedly gone out of their way to twist facts and to distort the political realities of the Middle East by insisting that Osama bin Laden's group's murderous attacks had nothing to do with Israel's policies towards the Palestinians. But even Britain, Bush's staunchest ally, linked Israel's intransigence towards negotiations and human rights violations as having contributed to the environment for Arab terrorist retaliation.

In late September 2001, a few days after the terrorist attacks in the US, during his visit to Jerusalem, British Foreign Secretary Jack Straw admitted that frustration over the Israel-Palestinian conflict might create an excuse for terrorism. Straw explained, 'there is never any excuse for terrorism. At the same time, there is an obvious need to understand the environment in which terrorism breeds'. Millions of moderate and progressive Muslims who sincerely denounce terrorism are nevertheless frustrated by the United States' extensive clientele relationship with Israel, financed by more than $ 3 billion in annual subsidies. They want to know why the US allowed the Israelis to move over 200,000 Jewish settlers – one half of them after the signing of the peace agreement, which was the result of the assurance by the US to Arab countries during the Gulf War – to relocate in occupied Palestine.

The US has a history of arrogantly rejecting its international obligations. One does not have to go into the long list of violations of international law by the US over the decades. Suffice it to point out a few instances in the period immediately preceding September 11. The US opposed the formation of an international criminal court under the auspices of the United Nations, but later signed the treaty. When the Court was constituted, after the War on Terror had begun, it withdrew its signature. The Bush administration withdrew from the important Kyoto treaty on climate change. The US boycotted the UN Conference Against Racism held in Durban, South Africa.

Many see a direct link between the terrible events of September 11 and the politics represented by the United Nations Conference in Durban only days prior to the terrorist attacks. The US government opposed the definition of slavery as a 'crime against humanity'. It refused to acknowledge the historical and contemporary effects of colonialism, racial segregation and apartheid on the underdevelopment and oppression of the non-European world. It polemically manipulated the charge of anti-Semitism to evade discussions concerning the right of self-determination for the Palestinian people. The world's subaltern masses represented at Durban sought to advance a new global discussion about the political economy of racism – and the United States insulted the entire international community.[11]

According to Marwan Bishara, 'If we just take a look at

the last year there is a general feeling around the world that America tends to pull out from important forums where disadvantaged people try to voice their claims and try to come to agreement with America and the West.'[12]

Jonathan Power wrote on September 12, 2001, a day after 9/11:

> The American nation appears not only immensely distressed and angry about the bombings but surprised too. . . . An event of this magnitude was not only unimagined, it was unimaginable. Yet long before George Bush became President with his forceful in-your-face, take-it-or-leave it attitude to the world on issues as diverse as global warming and anti-missile defences, America has been turning in on itself, to the point of self-destructiveness.
>
> I have talked to a range of ordinary Europeans in the last 24 hours and they all say, in the face of the earnest shoulder-to-shoulder rhetoric of their leaders, that America has got itself into this hold by its own disregard of what others think.
>
> America is threatened not by nuclear tipped missiles from unknown rogue nations, but by small groups of angry men, who, although prisoners of their zealotry, know well enough that much of the world whilst not agreeing with them understands their frustration. To deal with this effectively requires a new way of looking at the world.[13]

It is important how the events of September 11 are assessed. The War on Terror is America's response to it. An evaluation of September 11 will help in determining whether war is the right response. It will help in understanding whether there is justification for the nature, scope and strategy of the US war. Was there an alternative to the War on Terror? A proper assessment of that day is therefore very relevant. From that fateful day onwards

American and other Western leaders and media claimed that it was the beginning of a new chapter in history. Stanley Hoffman provides a corrective:

> As soon as the shock of the terror attacks on New York and Washington was felt, commentators began saying that September 11, 2001 marked the beginning of a new era in world affairs. It is a misleading interpretation of a horrible event. What was new was the demonstration that a small number of well-organized conspirators could cause thousands of victims in the territory of the 'only superpower' and thus show that the US was not any safer from attack than far less mighty nations. But the change of scale and the location of the targets do not represent a transformation of international relations.[14]

It is however a different matter that the events of that day were utilized by the US to change the world. The response to September 11 came in the form of a project to reorder the world using the military might of the USA, a project that was already under preparation. When it is claimed that the attack on September 11 in New York and Washington constitutes the greatest tragedy in the world and that it is an assault on justice, freedom and democracy all over the world, the necessary historical perspective and sense of proportion in evaluating events are ignored. It is claimed that the experience of the United States is of universal significance. In such a view, the US becomes the centre of the universe and what happens there ought to be therefore a matter of concern for the whole universe.

This universalist claim is made by the US, which, as pointed out earlier, has repeatedly turned its back arrogantly on its international obligations. The US has repeatedly declared that it does not care what happens to the rest of the world, it is not interested in such matters and it is not willing to listen to the grievances or demands or problems of others. It's own problem, however, is expected to be the problem of the whole world.

When hundreds of thousands of people died in Hiroshima and Nagasaki as a result of America's atom bombs, that was Japan's problem. When thousands of children die every year in Iraq as a result of sanctions, that is Iraq's problem. When tens of thousands of people die in Rwanda, it is their problem. Any tragedy in any country is that country's problem. But when some three thousand people are killed in the US, it is supposed to be the whole world's problem. This universalist claim tends to relativize and trivialize the histories, destinies and tragedies of other nations and peoples.

The events of September 11 demolished many of the assumptions of America's New World Order. The calculations about security, nature of threats, defence, weaponry, strategies, all went wrong. The Pentagon thought it knew from which direction and in which form attacks would come. The National Missile Defence was to be America's guarantee for national security. The weaknesses in this architecture of defence were beginning to be exposed much before September 11. But the attack on that day gave a body blow to America's belief system on security of the New World Order.

President Bush claims that the war he is leading now is the first war in the twenty-first century. It is useful, however, to recall Eric Hobsbawm's analysis in his book *The Short Twentieth Century*. Hobsbawm argues that the twentieth century was a short one and the twenty-first century began already in 1991. The devastating high tech war waged against Iraq by a grand coalition led by the US in 1991 was in the name of a New World Order. Armaments and strategies that would ensure zero casualties for Americans in wars formed part of this New World Order. The new NATO doctrine adopted on the occasion of the fiftieth anniversary of the organization, which claimed that NATO had the right to intervene in any part of the world politically, and if necessary militarily, in case there were developments or problems that affected the interests of the West, also was part of the New World Order. The war on terror is an imperialist war to make the world secure for the global economic and strategic interests of the United States.

Notes

1 Moises Naim, 'Why the World Loves to Hate America?' *Financial Times*, December 7, 2001.
2 Ibid.
3 Ibid.
4 Ibid.
5 Samuel P. Huntington, *The Clash of Civilizations and the Remaking of World Order*, Simon & Schuster, 1996.
6 Samuel P. Huntington, 'The Age of Muslim Wars', *Newsweek*, Davos Special Edition, December 2000 to February 2001.
7 Ibid.
8 See www.zmag.org/saidclash.htm.
9 Andrew Johnston, 'Disparities in Wealth are seen as Fuel for Terrorism', *International Herald Tribune*, December 19, 2001.
10 Quoted in ibid.
11 Manning Marable, 'The Failure of US Foreign Policies', www.tni.org/wtc/documents/marable.htm.
12 Quoted by Andrew Johnston, 'Disparities in Wealth'.
13 Jonathan Power, 'For the Arrogance of Power America Now Pays a Terrible Price,' *Jonathan Power Forum*, September 12, 2001.
14 Stanley Hoffman, 'On the War', *New York Review of Books*, November 1, 2001.

3

'Terrorism: Theirs and Ours'

The United States declared War on Terror in the wake of the terrorist attacks of September 11. The US claimed it had evidence that the World Trade Centre and the Pentagon were attacked by Al Qaeda, an organization under the leadership of Osama bin Laden. While there is no doubt that the attacks on September 11 were terrorist attacks, it is not easy to define terrorism, terrorist activity or a terrorist organization. While the United Nations has made several important declarations against terrorism and initiated political and legal steps against it, its attempts to give a definition to terrorism has not succeeded. Nations and individuals view terrorism in different ways. A nation might revise its own earlier understanding of terrorism and its list of terrorist organizations as circumstances change.

The concept of 'terrorism' has been a category of political discourse since the late eighteenth century but has been especially prominent since the 1970s. Very broadly, it refers to the use of terror for the furthering of political ends. The term was originally used to denote the use of terror by the French revolutionary government against its opponents. This is also the sense in which it was used, and on occasion justified, by the Bolsheviks after 1917. This usage of the term, to cover terror by governments, has now become less common, although by no means irrelevant, and in most contemporary usage the term covers acts of terror by those opposed to governments. The range of activities which the term covers has been wide, but four main forms of action tend to be included: assassinations, bombings, seizures of individuals as hostages, and the hijacking of planes. In the 1970s the term 'international terrorism' began to be used to cover acts of violence committed by political groups outside the country in which they were primarily active. The other term that emerged at the same time, 'state terrorism', referred to encouragement, or alleged encouragement, by states of such acts of violence.[1]

To say that one person's terrorist is another person's freedom fighter is not a cliché but a statement of fact which underlines the difficulty in defining 'terrorism' and 'terrorist'. Militants in Kashmir are terrorists to the government of India but to Pakistan they are freedom fighters. Hamas and Hizbulla are terrorist organisations to the US and Israel but they are liberation movements to vast sections of people. Those who were once labelled terrorists later became leaders of nations and heads of states, and 'terrorist' organizations became ruling parties. Taking into account such changes, other nations and the media accordingly revised their attitudes to them. For instance, once the US and many other Western nations officially termed liberation movements like the African National Congress terrorist organizations.

The well-known Pakistani intellectual Eqbal Ahmad made a fascinating and penetrating analysis of terrorism in a speech entitled 'Terrorism: Theirs and Ours' at the University of Colorado, Boulder, on October 12, 1998:

> In the 1930s and 1940s, the Jewish underground in Palestine was described as 'terrorist'. Then new things happened. By 1942 the Holocaust was occurring, and a certain liberal sympathy with the Jewish people had built up in the Western world. At that point, the terrorists of Palestine, who were Zionists, suddenly

started to be described by 1944–45 as 'freedom fighters'.

Then from 1969 to 1990 the PLO, the Palestine Liberation Organization, occupied the centre stage as the terrorist organization.

In 1985 President Ronald Reagan received a group of bearded men. They were very ferocious looking bearded men with turbans, looking like they came from another country. President Regan received them in the White House. After receiving them he spoke to the press. He pointed towards them and said 'These are the moral equivalent of America's founding fathers.' They were the Afghan Mujaheddin. They were at the time, guns in hand, battling the Evil Empire.

In August 1998, another American President ordered missile strikes from the American navy based in the Indian Ocean to kill Osama bin Laden and his men in the camps in Afghanistan. I do not wish to embarrass you with the reminder that Mr bin Laden, whom fifteen American missiles were fired to hit in Afghanistan, was only a few years ago the moral equivalent of George Washington and Thomas Jefferson.

You see, why I have recalled all these stories is to point out to you that the matter of terrorism is rather complicated. Terrorists change. The terrorist of yesterday is the hero of today. This is a serious matter of the constantly changing world of images in which we have to keep our heads straight to know what is terrorism and what is not. But more importantly, to know what causes it, and how to stop it.[2]

Ahmad points out that the moral revulsion that the United States shows against terrorism is selective. 'We are to feel the terror of those groups, which are officially disapproved. We are to applaud the terror of those groups of whom officials do approve. Hence, President Reagan, "I am contra". He actually said that'.[3]

Rather than define terrorism, a number of people describe it emotively and polemically to arouse emotions rather than exercise intelligence. In 1984, George Shultz, then US Secretary of State, made a long speech on terrorism at the New York Park Avenue Synagogue. He described terrorism variously as: 'Terrorism is a modern barbarism we call terrorism', 'Terrorism is a form of political violence', 'Terrorism is a threat to Western civilization', 'Terrorism is a menace to Western moral values'. Interestingly, already in 1984, Shultz claimed that the fight against terrorism had to be global: 'There is no question about our ability to use force where and when it needs to counter terrorism'. Anticipating the easy certainty of the present administration, Shultz claimed to have no difficulty in identifying terrorists. 'We know the difference between terrorists and freedom fighters, and as we look around we have no trouble telling one from the other.'[4] These views are important, since it is Shultz's doctrine of 'hot pre-emption' that is currently shaping Washington's strategy in the War on Terror.

Jeff Cohen exposes the double standards in defining terrorists:

> 1. Terrorist. *One who engages in acts or an act of terrorism.*
>
> 2. One who leads an armed group that kills civilians as a means of political intimidation – *unless he terrorizes Haitians while on the CIA-payroll as did 1990s death squad leader Emmanuel Constant in which case the US refuses to extradite him to Haiti, even after September 11, 2001.*
>
> 3. One who targets civilian airliners and ships – *unless he blows up a Cuban civilian airliner, killing 73 people, and fires at a Polish freighter, like Orlando Boach in which case he is coddled and paroled by the Bush Justice Department in 1990, and his extradition is blocked.*

4. One who leads a group that engages in kidnapping and murder – *unless the victims are Hondurans attacked by CIA-backed death squad Battalion 316, in which case Battalion architect Gustavo Alvarez becomes a Pentagon consultant while the then-ambassador who downplayed the terror, John Negroponte, is appointed US ambassador to the United Nations days after September 11.*

5. One who designates civilians as 'soft targets' to be attacked in the cause of political transformation – *unless the targets are Nicaraguans killed by contra guerrillas armed and directed by the US who, according to Human Rights Watch 'systematically engage in violent abuses . . . so prevalent that they may be said to be their principal means of waging war.'*

6. One who facilitates a massacre of civilians – *unless the victims are 900 Palestinians shot and hacked to death in the Sabra and Shatilla camps by Lebanese Christian militia as Israel's then-Defence Minister (now Prime Minister) Ariel Sharon remains a US 'War on Terror' ally after being censured as indirectly responsible for the massacre by an Israeli commission of inquiry.*[5]

Notwithstanding such hypocrisy, it is nonetheless easier to *understand* a terrorist act than to *define* terrorism or a terrorist. Attack on innocent people is a terrorist act. Targeting mainly civilians and non-combatants is a terrorist act. Such terrorist acts are carried out by states, some state agencies, some organizations and sections of some organizations. Whoever perpetrates them, attacks mainly targeting civilians can be termed terrorist acts. Killing of civilians in the course of an attack not mainly directed against them raises other questions.

Usually the term terrorism is applied to organizations and individuals. But there are many states which deserve to be labelled terrorist. For the security of people inside a country, a state may have to resort to force and military power against attack from outside. Coercion may have to be used inside a country for maintaining peace and order. But if a state, outside or inside a nation, transgresses the limits and laws regarding legitimate use of force and targets innocent people, this should be termed 'state terrorism'.

Terrorism is attack targeted mainly against civilians. There are laws of war. In the Second World War both the sides violated the laws of war. The greatest such violation, however, occurred when the US dropped atom bombs in Hiroshima and Nagasaki. It was an act of nuclear terror. The act was not necessary either to end the war or to make the Japanese surrender. It was not a military mission. Those who were attacked were civilians. There are many instances of a state making terrorist attacks against its own people – Indonesia, Uganda, Kampuchea, Guatemala, are only some examples. The terrorist acts in Lebanon in 1982 and the role of Ariel Sharon have already been referred to.

Terrorism does not help the cause of freedom or justice. Therefore terrorism cannot be part of the struggle for freedom or liberation. In fact terrorism can endanger freedom and justice and counter-productively encourage reactionary forces. The taking up of arms for defence by a liberation movement with a wide popular base at some defined stage of the struggle is not terrorism. Indeed, there may be armed struggles which can be justified. But they too have limits and criteria. When they are violated such actions tend to be terrorist.

John Berger argues that 'The US nuclear attack on Hiroshima paved the way for September 11 and its aftermath.'

> When on September 11, I watched the videos on television, I was instantly reminded of August 6, 1945. The immediate correspondences between the two events include a fireball descending without warning from a clear sky, both attacks being

> timed to coincide with the civilians of the targeted city going to work in the morning, with the shops opening, with children in school preparing their lessons. A similar reduction to ashes, with bodies, flung through the air, becoming debris. A comparable incredulity and chaos provoked by a new weapon of destruction being used for the first time – the A-bomb 60 years ago, and a civil airliner last autumn. Everywhere at the epicentre, on everything and everybody, a thick pall of dust.
>
> The differences of content and scale are of course enormous. In Manhattan the dust was not radioactive. . . . Both attacks, however, were planned as announcements. . . . The bombs dropped on Hiroshima and Nagasaki announced that the US was henceforth the supreme armed power in the world. The attack of September 11 announced that this power was no longer guaranteed invulnerability on its home ground.[6]

Is there any difference between revolutionary terror and what we know as terrorism? Eqbal Ahmad makes the point that the 'absence of revolutionary ideology is central to victim terrorism':

> Revolutionaries do not commit unthinking terror. Those of you who are familiar with revolutionary theory know the debates, the disputes, the quarrels, the fights within revolutionary groups of Europe, the fight between anarchists and Marxists, for example. But the Marxists have always argued that revolutionary terror, if ever engaged in, must be sociologically and psychologically selective. Don't hijack a plane. Don't hold hostages. Don't kill children, for God's sake. Have you recalled also that the great revolutions, the Chinese, the Vietnamese, the Algerian, the Cuban, never engaged in hijacking type of terrorism? They did engage in terrorism, but it was highly selective, highly sociological, still deplorable, but there was an organized, highly limited

> selective character to it. So absence of revolutionary ideology that begins more or less in the post-World War II period has been central to the phenomenon.[7]

Some of the ambiguities in dealing with the issue of terrorism are brought to the fore in an article by Grenville Byford.[8] 'Terrorists, it is usually agreed, are defined not by their goal but by how they elect to pursue them. If terrorism is never to be countenanced, terrorists must employ some means that no end can justify. But how exactly are unjustifiable means to be identified?' Byford takes up the question of killing of civilians.

> Are terrorists those who deliberately set out to kill civilians? This inquiry raises the politically incorrect question of what is wrong with killing civilians. Civilians are not always mere bystanders and are crucial to any war effort. US military power is based on America's economic success. This relationship holds for any halfway modern economy and provides the justification for attacking industrial targets in a war – whether in Hamburg half a century ago, or in Belgrade recently. The United States, furthermore, is a democracy; its citizens help decide how its military power is used. . . . Are they truly innocent? . . . Serbs under Slobadan Milosevic and Iraqis under Saddam Hussein, some of whom must have had a better claim on the word 'innocent' than the citizens of democratic America, have been killed in recent years by American bombs.

Byford's remarks on the moral dilemma are pertinent:

> And consider the case of those opposing a government so ruthless and powerful that any attack on its armed forces is tantamount to suicide. Can we say that in such a situation no armed struggle

> against the regime is legitimate, since the opposition would have to employ force against civilian targets and would certainly kill the innocent? The sad truth is that for many people – some of them decent – a scrupulously honourable struggle is an unaffordable luxury. Recognizing this reality, most of us will not pass judgement on any combatants without also considering the ends they pursue. . . . How much moral latitude should be allowed is an issue about which reasonable people can differ. The argument, however, will generally centre not merely on the morality of the tactics themselves but on the justice of the cause and the nature of the alternatives possible. Few statues are built in remembrance of people who fought honourably for a rotten cause, most celebrate those made moral compromises for a good one. Ends and means are hopelessly conflated.

Is motivation an important issue in terrorism? A US statutory definition of terrorism [22USC 2656 f (d)], frequently cited, defines terrorism as premeditated politically motivated violence against non-combatants by groups or individuals, usually intended to influence an audience. However, as Raphael Perl explains,

> there appears to be a growing pragmatic trend in (US) policy circles to define terrorism by the nature of the act and not the motivation behind it. Pushing such definitional criteria to the limit, it becomes immaterial whether or not motivation is 'political'. Also under such new definitional criteria, the form of 'violence' employed can be non-traditional such as a cyber attack. Inherent in such an evolving definitional framework is recognition that a terrorist can be defined in terms which go beyond traditional concepts of physical injury, destruction and fear to include grave economic damage. This dovetails with the avowed

objectives of a network like Al Qaeda, which see attacking America's economy and the global economic system as central objectives.[9]

Perl notes how American perceptions of terrorism changed:

> Before the events of September 11th, the public in the United States primarily viewed terrorism as an overseas issue. True, Americans and American interests were seen as target, but not on American soil. Today, for Americans, terrorism is seen as a threat to our security inside the territory of the United States. Moreover, before September 11th, many Americans perceived terrorism as primarily a law enforcement issue. Today most perceive it as a national security threat as well with potential for mass casualties and widespread havoc and destruction. Before September 11th, Americans largely perceived the threat of terrorism as a foreign grown and based phenomenon. Only now are we beginning a process which seriously grapples with the thought that, in the future, the United States may see more instances of the 'home grown' variety of terrorism.

However there is no evidence that American perceptions about terrorism before or after September 11 are shared across the world. Countries which joined the grand coalition against terrorism had their own views on terrorism and terrorists. They were not all agreed that they were fighting an international threat.

'In the United States, however, there is no question that terrorism is a transnational threat', says Ehsan Ahrari.

> How to deal with it is an issue on which there are two schools of thought: the 'middle-grounders' and the 'eradicators'. The first group argues for developing a whole panoply of solutions, from

> political to diplomatic, and military. The eradicators, on the contrary, have a straightforward hawkish approach to transnational terrorism: hit them, wherever they are, no questions asked, since it is known who they are. They also seem to be saying, 'We don't need affirmation from allies, nor any debates. If whacking of the terrorists has to be done unilaterally, so be it.'[10]

In Washington the 'middle-grounders' are fast losing even the little ground they had and the 'eradicators' are reigning supreme. Ahrari continues:

> The greatest challenge the Bush administration faces on global terrorism is that all countries of the world condemn it, but only a few are willing to adopt the US type of voluble perspective on that issue, which is an intermingling of militarism and highfalutin moralism. These two characteristics of America's rhetoric have no takers in the Middle East, save Israel, all takers in the highly repressive Central Asian republics, since the sole motivation of the corrupt rulers in these countries is to extend the tenure of their unjust rule, and a few tentative takers, save the UK, in Europe. Russia and China are supporting it for very specific reasons of suppressing their own secessionist groups – the Chechens and the Ughur – whose depiction as 'terrorists' is not at all a widely shared perspective outside their borders.

The East Asian countries, though they are sympathetic to the US on the need to tackle terrorism, are not interested in maintaining a high profile along those lines. Obviously Australia is an exception to that observation. In the case of Indonesia, which is a fledgling democracy, anti-US sentiments are so intense that President Megawati Sukarnoputri thought it best to keep a low profile on her government's policy against terrorism – condemning it in principle but not actively engaged in suppressing it for fear of deleterious and potentially destabilising backlash. In South Asia, India and Pakistan are supporting the US perspective on terrorism for reasons that are entirely regional and, inter-alia, are also related to the obdurate Kashmir conflict.

Each nation is looking at terrorism and terrorists through the prism of its own national situation and interests. The war on terror is an American enterprise for which support will be forthcoming from nations to the extent it helps them deal with 'their own terrorists'.

Notes

1 Fred Halliday, 'Terrorism', Global Policy Forum, May 2001.
2 Eqbal Ahmad, 'Terrorism: Theirs and Ours', available at www.tni.org/wtc/documents/ahmad.htm.
3 Ibid.
4 Quoted by Ahmad, ibid.
5 Jeff Cohen, 'What is a Terrorist?', *Commondreams,* May 1, 2002.
6 John Berger, 'The First Fireball,' *The Guardian of London,* June 29, 2002.
7 Ahmad, 'Terrorism: Theirs and Ours'.
8 Grenwille Byford, *Foreign Affairs,* July-August 2002.
9 Raphael Perl, Address to German Council on Foreign Relations, *International Information Programs,* State Department, July 2, 2002.
10 Ehsan Ahrari, 'Divergent Views on the Common Scourge of Terror', *Asia Times,* June 27, 2002.

4

Arab-Afghans on the Centre Stage

In his address to the joint session of the Congress on September 20, 2001, President Bush identified Al Qaeda as the perpetrators of the terrorist attacks on September 11 and accused Afghanistan and its rulers Taliban of harbouring Osama bin Laden.

A brief look into the history of Afghanistan may be helpful in locating Al Qaeda and Taliban.

Fighting foreign aggressors for centuries, Afghanistan was unified in 1747. During the nineteenth century it was repeatedly invaded by Britain as part of the 'Great Game' for control over Central Asia. London never succeeded in gaining control over the country, which eventually wrested full independence for itself in the aftermath of the First World War. During the Cold War both sides wooed Afghanistan, which made significant territorial claims against Pakistan.

In 1973, a military coup abolished the monarchy and established a republic. Ensuing reforms ushered in a period of political instability. Two more violent coups by different communist factions in 1978 and 1979 helped provoke Islamic insurgencies and finally a Soviet military intervention in December 1979.

In the decade that followed, fighting between Soviet and Afghan government troops against Mujaheddin guerrillas backed by Pakistan, the US, and Saudi Arabia devastated the country. Moscow withdrew in 1989, leaving President Najibullah to fight on alone. In early 1992, the Mujaheddin coalition captured Kabul but quickly proved unable to sustain its unity amid fighting between ethnic-based factions. A new civil war ensued this time among the different factions and warlords that constituted the Mujaheddin. The Northern Alliance had the upper hand for a time.

In late 1994, the Taliban, a Pakistan-backed militia consisting of Pashtun Islamic fundamentalists, launched operations along the Pakistani border, sweeping westward until it finally captured Kabul in September 1996. In 1998, the UN Security Council imposed economic sanctions against the Taliban for its refusal to turn over Osama bin Laden in connection with attacks on US embassies in Kenya and Tanzania. In March 1999, the United Nations brokered a cease-fire between the Taliban and the Northern Alliance forces under Ahmed Shah Massoud, an ethnic Tajik, but fighting resumed in July. In December 2000, the Security Council imposed a ban on arms sales to the Taliban.

A combination of crippling drought, shortfalls in humanitarian aid and continued international isolation – compounded by the Taliban's destruction of famous Buddhist statues throughout Afghanistan – contributed to growing hunger and a new outflow of refugees. In September 2001, tensions mounted sharply after Massoud, the Northern Alliance's chief military commander, was assassinated. The terrorist attacks on the World Trade Centre towers in New York and Pentagon outside Washington, DC, came soon after that.

The targets of the US military action in Afghanistan – which continues even after the Taliban have been ousted from Kabul – are Taliban and Al Qaeda. But in the extensive official documentation of the administration on the war on terror, one finds no coherent explanation of the origins of these organizations, their social and ideological base, and their rise to power and influence. The omission is no accident because any serious examination of these organizations will reveal the culpability of Washington in fostering them.

The year was 1986. The Central Intelligence Agency (CIA) chief William Casey decided to step up the Afghan war against the Soviet Union. He took three significant, but at that time highly secret, measures. He persuaded the US Congress to provide the Mujaheddin with American-made Stinger anti-aircraft missiles to shoot down Soviet planes. He succeeded in persuading the Congress to provide US advisers to train the guerrillas. Until then no US weapons or personnel had been used directly in the war effort. The second decision took the war to a new stage. The CIA, Britain's M16 and Pakistan's Inter-Service Intelligence (ISI) also agreed on a provocative plan to launch guerrilla attacks into the Soviet Socialist Republics of Tajikistan and Uzbekistan, from where Soviet troops received their supplies. This task was given to the ISI's favourite Mujaheddin leader Gulbuddin Hekmetyar.

The third decision was the most far-reaching. Casey committed CIA support to a long-standing initiative of Pakistan's ISI to recruit radical Muslims from around the world to come to Pakistan and fight with the Mujaheddin. Ahmed Rashid, the correspondent who has covered the region for a long time, notes:

> The ISI had encouraged this since 1982 and by now all the other players had their reasons for supporting the idea. Pakistan's President Zia wanted to forge a new Islamic unity, make Pakistan the leader of the Muslim world and foster an Islamic opposition in Central Asia. Washington wanted to show that it was supporting an enterprise of the entire Muslim world fighting the Soviet Union. The Saudis saw an opportunity to export the country's disgruntled radicals and in the bargain to promote Wahabbism. The intelligence agencies of these countries or their political masters did not anticipate that those volunteers will

> shape their own agendas which would turn them against their sponsors after they dealt with the Soviets.[1]

It is estimated that between 1982 and 1992 some 35,000 Muslim radicals from 43 Islamic countries in the Middle East, North and East Africa, Central Asia and the Far East were trained under the Mujaheddin. Tens of thousands more foreign Muslim radicals came to study in the hundreds of new *madrassas* (schools) that Zia's military government began to fund in Pakistan and along the Afghan border. Eventually more than 100,000 Muslim radicals were to have direct contact with Pakistan and Afghanistan and be influenced by jihad. French scholar Olivier Roy described it as 'a joint venture between the Saudis, the Muslim Brotherhood and the Jamait-e-Islami put together by the ISI'.[2]

In camps near Peshawar and in Afghanistan, these radicals studied and trained, and forged tactical and ideological links that would serve them well in the future. These camps became universities and defence colleges of Islamic fundamentalism. It appears that none of the intelligence agencies which sponsored them considered the implications and consequences of bringing together Islamic radicals from all over the world. As Samuel Huntington puts it,

> The war left behind an uneasy coalition of Islamic organizations intent on promoting Islam against all non-Muslim forces. It also left a legacy of experts and experienced fighters, training camps and logistical facilities, elaborate trans-Islam networks of personal and organization relationships, a substantial amount of military equipment including 300 to 500 unaccounted-for Stinger missiles and most important, a heady sense of power and self-confidence over what had been achieved and a driving desire to move on to other victories.[3]

Ahmed Rashid explains the consequences of this 'heady sense of power' and 'a driving desire to move on to other victories':

> Most of these radicals speculated that if the Afghan jihad had defeated one superpower, the Soviet Union, could they not also defeat the other superpower, the US and their own regimes. The logic of this argument was based on the simple premise that the Afghan jihad alone brought the Soviet state to its knees. The multiple internal reasons, which led to the collapse of the Soviet system, of which the jihad was only one, were conveniently ignored. So while the USA saw the collapse of the Soviet State as the failure of communism, many Muslims saw it solely as a victory for Islam. For militants this belief was inspiring and deeply evocative of the Muslim sweep across the world in the seventh and eighth centuries. A new Islamic *Ummah,* they argued, could be forged by the sacrifice and blood of a new generation of martyrs and more such victories.[4]

Osama bin Laden came to the scene as one among the thousands of young foreign recruits. His father was a Yemeni construction magnate Mohammed bin Laden who had close connections with the Saudi royal family. The elder bin Laden supported the Afghan struggle and helped fund it. So Osama had the enthusiastic support of his family. Bin Laden was a star recruit for the Mujaheddin. The Mujaheddin actually wanted a prince from the Saudi royal family. With all the connections that bin Laden had, he was as good as a member of the royal family. He first went to Peshawar in 1980 and met the Mujaheddin leaders. Then he frequently visited them with Saudi donations for the cause until 1982 when he decided to settle down in Peshawar. Rashid describes how

> He brought in his company engineers and heavy construction equipment to help build roads and depots for the Mujaheddin. In 1986 he helped build the Khost tunnel complex, which the CIA was funding as a major arms storage depot, training facility and medical centre for the Mujaheddin, deep under the mountains close to the Pakistani border. For the first time in Khost he set up his own training camp for Arab Afghans, who now increasingly saw this lanky, wealthy and charismatic Saudi as their leader.[5]

Al Qaeda or Military Base was set up as a service centre for Arab-Afghans and their families and to forge a broad-based alliance against the Russians. In Osama bin Laden's own words,

> To counter these atheist Russians, the Saudis chose me as their representative in Afghanistan. I settled in Pakistan in the Afghan border region. There I received volunteers who came from the Saudi kingdom and from all over the Arab and Muslim countries. I set up my first camp where these volunteers were trained by Pakistani and American officers. The weapons were supplied by the Americans, the money by the Saudis. I discovered that it was not enough to fight in Afghanistan, but that we had to fight on all fronts, communist or Western oppression.[6]

By 1990 bin Laden was disillusioned by the internal bickering of the Mujaheddin and he returned to Saudi Arabia to work on the family business. He founded a welfare organization for Arab-Afghan veterans. After Iraq's invasion of Kuwait he lobbied the royal family to organize a popular defence of the Kingdom and raise a force from the Afghan war veterans to fight Iraq. Rejecting bin Laden's proposal, the King invited the Americans. As more than five hundred thousand US troops began to arrive in the Kingdom, bin Laden openly criticized the royal family and lobbied the Saudi *ulema* to issue *fatwas* (religious rulings) against non-Muslims in the country. When bin Laden escalated his criticism as more than twenty thousand American troops continued to stay in Saudi Arabia even after the liberation of Kuwait, it became clear that the government would initiate action against him.

In 1992 bin Laden left for Sudan to take part in the Islamic revolution underway there under the charismatic leadership of Hassan Al Turabi. The highly intelligent and articulate Al Turabi had by then become the ideologue of Islamic fundamentalism and he had great influence in the military government of Sudan. The patronage of Al Turabi was fully utilized by bin Laden. It was in Sudan, with his wealth and contacts, that bin Laden gathered around him more veterans of the Afghan war, who were all disgusted by the American victory over Iraq and the attitude of the Arab ruling elite who allowed the US military to remain in the Gulf. The Americans and the Saudis mounted pressure against Sudan for harbouring bin Laden, finally forcing the Sudanese authorities to ask him to leave. Even Turabi could not help him any longer.

In May 1996 bin Laden returned to Afghanistan. Here he lived under the protection of the Jalalabad Shura until the conquest of Kabul and Jalalabad by the Taliban in September 1996.

The Soviet-backed regime of Mohammad Najibullah had managed to survive till 1992. By the time it fell, Kabul had become a battleground for competing Mujaheddin militias. Burhanuddin Rabbani, the nominal head of a government presided over a highly unstable and shifting coalition, based mainly on ethnic Tajiks and Uzbeks from northern Afghanistan. The rival Hizb-e-Islami militia, drawn from the Pashtun majority in southern Afghanistan, was also entrenched in the suburbs of Kabul. Led by Gulbuddin Hekmetyar, it was subjecting government positions in the capital to an intensive rocket barrage. A number of other militia groups under warlords representing the country's myriad of ethnic and religious divisions were also fighting, taking one side or the other and sometimes changing sides. The capital was devastated, producing wave after wave of refugees. In addition to local factors and interests behind these groups were also the interests of several states. Hekmatyar was for long supported by Pakistan. Iran backed the Shiite Hazaras. Saudi Arabia had its own groups particularly those sympathetic to its brand of Islam – Wahabbism. The Central Asian republics had connections to the ethnic groups in Northern Afghanistan and, in the background, India, Russia and the US all had a hand in Afghan political affairs.

The Pashtun areas in the south, where the Taliban emerged in 1994, were among the most chaotic. Kandahar, the country's second largest city, was divided between three rival warlords, and the surrounding areas were subject to the arbitrary and often brutal rule of dozens of militia commanders. The region, which was one of Afghanistan's most economically backward and socially conservative, had traditionally provided the country's royal rulers. Local resentment over the new Tajik and Uzbek rulers in Kabul was compounded by the desperation produced by the worsening economic and social conditions.

The rather sudden emergence of the Taliban on the Afghan scene surprised many observers. The rapidity of its growth and success was even more astonishing. Two factors were responsible for this: firstly, the social and political quagmire that produced a ready supply of recruits, and secondly, external aid from Pakistan, Saudi Arabia, and in all likelihood the US, in the form of finance, arms and advisers.

Although a number of Taliban leaders had fought in the US-sponsored jihad against the Soviet Union, the movement was not a breakaway from, or an amalgamation of, other Mujaheddin factions. It was largely based on a new generation who had not been directly involved in the fighting of the 1980s. They were hostile to what they saw as the corrupt rule of petty Mujaheddin despots who had brought nothing but misery to the lives of ordinary Afghans in the wake of Najibullah's fall. Their own lives had been torn apart by war. Many of them had grown up in the refugee camps inside Pakistan and received a rudimentary education in the *madrassas* run by various Pakistani Islamic extremist parties. Ahmed Rashid provides the following description:

> These boys were from a generation who had never seen their country at peace – an Afghanistan not at war with invaders and itself. . . . They were literally orphans of the war, the rootless and the restless, the jobless and the economically deprived with little self-knowledge. Their simple belief in a messianic puritan Islam which had been drummed into them by simple village mullahs was the only prop they had to hold on to and which gave their lives some meaning.[7]

From the outset, the movement was profoundly reactionary. It looked backward for solutions of social problems to a mythical past when the precepts of the prophet Mohammad were strictly observed. Its leaders were semi-educated village mullahs, not learned Islamic scholars versed in the scriptures and religious commentaries. They were hostile to other Islamic sects, particularly the Shias, and to non-Pashtun ethnic groups. In as much as their ideology had an Islamic base, it was Deobandism – an influential nineteenth-century reform movement – but in a form that was devoid of anything remotely progressive.

From the outset, the Taliban's sponsor was Pakistan's powerful ISI, which had been the principal conduit for US money, arms and expertise to the Mujaheddin groups throughout the 1980s, and which was deeply enmeshed in Afghan politics. But in the new dispensation after the fall of Najibullah, Pakistan's proxy

Hekmatyar, bogged down in fighting in Kabul, provided no solace or solution to his patron. It was then in September 1994, that the Benazir Bhutto government hit upon the idea of using the Taliban to oust the Northern Alliance-led Kabul regime.

Over the next three months, the Taliban took control of 12 of Afghanistan's 31 provinces. At least some of its 'victories' were secured with large bribes and other inducements to local militia commanders and warlords. After suffering military reversals in mid-1995, the Taliban rearmed and reorganized with Pakistani assistance and in September 1995 entered Herat, effectively clearing the road from Pakistan to Central Asia.

It was clear that the Taliban success was not because of the magic of its ideology or popular support but substantial support from outside. The most telling sign of external involvement was its stunning military victories. In little more than a year, it had grown from a handful of *taliban* (students) to a well-organized militia that could muster up to 20,000 fighters, backed by tanks, artillery and air support, controlling large swathes of southern and western Afghanistan.

As Martin Ewers observed,

> It is also inconceivable that a force composed mostly of former guerrillas and student amateurs could have operated with the degree of skill and organization which the Taliban showed almost form the outset of their operations. While there were undoubtedly former members of the Afghani armed forces among their numbers, the speed and the sophistication with which their offensives were conducted, and the quality of such elements as their communications, air support and artillery bombardments, lead to the inescapable conclusion that they must have owed much to a Pakistani military presence or at least professional support.[8]

Pakistan was not the only source of assistance. Saudi Arabia also provided substantial financial and material aid. The Taliban's political ideology was close to the Saudi's own Wahabbism. Indirectly some support might have gone from the Americans too.

Like Pakistan and Saudi Arabia, the US has repeatedly denied any support for the Taliban. Given the close involvement of the CIA with Pakistan and the ISI throughout the 1980s, however, it is highly implausible that Washington did not know of and give tacit approval to, the Bhutto government's plans for the Taliban. Ahmed Rashid makes the following comment:

> The Clinton administration was clearly sympathetic to the Taliban, as they were in line with Washington's anti-Iran policy and were important for the success of any southern pipeline from Central Asia that would avoid Iran. The US Congress had authorized a covert $20 million budget for the CIA to destabilize Iran, and Tehran had accused Washington of funnelling some of these funds to the Taliban – a charge that was always denied by Washington.[9]

In August 1996, Taliban troops seized Jalalabad on the Pakistan border and finally forced opposition forces to withdraw from Kabul the following month.

> Within hours of Kabul's capture by the Taliban, the US State Department announced that it would establish diplomatic relations with the Taliban by sending an official to Kabul – an announcement quickly retracted. State Department spokesman Glyn Davies said the US found 'nothing objectionable' in the steps taken by the Taliban to impose Islamic law. He described the Taliban as anti-modern rather than anti-Western. US

Congressmen weighed in on the side of the Taliban. 'The good part of what has happened is that one of the factions at last seems capable of developing a government in Afghanistan,' said Senator Hank Brown, a supporter of the UNOCAL project.[10]

Rashid says,

> Embarrassed US diplomats later explained to me that the over-hasty US statement was made without consulting the US Embassy in Islamabad. But the damage done was enormous. UNOCAL's gaffes and the confusion in the State Department only further convinced Iran, Russia, the anti-Taliban alliance and most Pakistanis and Afghans that the US-UNOCAL partnership was backing the Taliban and wanted an all-out Taliban victory – even as the US and UNOCAL claimed they had no favourites in Afghanistan.[11]

Between 1994 and 1996 the USA supported the Taliban politically through its allies Pakistan and Saudi Arabia, essentially because Washington viewed the Taliban as anti-Iranian, anti-Shia and pro-Western. The USA conveniently ignored the Taliban's own Islamic fundamentalist agenda, its suppression of women and the consternation they created in Central Asia largely because Washington was not interested in the larger picture. Between 1995 and 1997 US support was even more driven because of its backing for the UNOCAL project.

Speaking in a closed-door session at a meeting convened by the UN in November 1996, US Assistant Secretary of State for South Asia Robin Raphel arduously defended Taliban:

> The Taliban control more than two-third of the country, they are Afghan, they are indigenous, they have demonstrated staying

> power. The real source of their success has been the willingness of many Afghans, particularly Pashtuns, to tacitly trade unending fighting and chaos for a measure of peace and security, even with severe social restrictions. It is not in the interests of Afghanistan or any of us here that the Taliban be isolated.[12]

But political developments in Afghanistan were already beginning to affect Washington's policies. The key turning point came in May 1997 when the Taliban regime captured the major northern city of Mazar-e-Sharif and attempted to impose their religious and social structures on a hostile and suspicious population of Uzbeks, Tajiks and Shiite Hazras. The actions provoked a revolt. The Taliban was driven back but it recaptured the city. These were bloody battles. They showed that the civil war would inevitably be a protracted one and even if the Taliban succeeded in taking the opposition strongholds in the north, rebellions and further political instability were likely. It was clear that the 'measure of peace and security' that Washington claimed could not be attained or sustained by Taliban.

The shift in Washington's political stance became public in November 1997. It was US Secretary of State Madeline Albright who set the new tone during a visit to Pakistan. She took the opportunity to denounce the Taliban's policies towards women as 'despicable' and to pointedly warn Pakistan that it risked international isolation. Washington began to exert pressure on Pakistan over the Taliban's involvement in the heroin trade and the dangers of 'Islamic terrorism.' The change in US policy became complete when, in the aftermath of the bombing of the US embassies in Kenya and Tanzania in August 1998, the Clinton administration launched cruise missiles against Osama bin Laden's training camps at Khost in Afghanistan.

In August 1996 Osama bin Laden had issued his first

declaration of jihad against the Americans who, he said, were occupying Saudi Arabia. 'The walls of opposition and humiliation cannot be demolished except in a rain of bullets', the declaration read. Striking up a friendship with Mullah Omar, the Taliban's supreme leader, in 1997 he moved to Kandahar and came under the protection of the Taliban.

It was the bombings in August 1998 of the US embassies in Kenya and Tanzania that killed 220 people, which made bin Laden a household name in the Muslim world and the West. Just 13 days later, after accusing bin Laden of perpetrating the attack, the US retaliated by firing 70 cruise missiles against bin Laden's camps around Khost and Jalalabad. Some 34 persons, belonging to different nationalities died. Bin Laden escaped.

In November 1998 the USA offered a $5 million reward for bin Laden's capture. A statement by bin Laden that it was his Islamic duty to acquire chemical and nuclear weapons for use against the US was taken seriously by President Clinton. In the shadow of the Monica Lewinsky scandal, the demonization of bin Laden was a welcome exercise for the President. The administration accused bin Laden of every atrocity committed against the US from the beginning of the 1990s. Bin Laden was blamed for the killing of 18 American soldiers in Mogadishu, Somalia in 1993, the deaths of five servicemen in a bomb attack in Riyadh in 1995, and the deaths of another 19 soldiers in Dhahran in 1996. He was also suspected of having a hand in bombings in Aden in 1992, the World Trade Centre bombing in 1993, the 1994 plot to kill President Clinton in the Philippines and a plan to blow up a dozen US civilian aircraft in 1995.[13] There was a great deal of scepticism, even amongst US experts that he was involved in many of these latter operations.[14]

What the administration failed to admit was its own role, mainly through the CIA, in creating the 'demon' that posed a threat not only to the United States but also to many countries including those from which members of the Al Qaeda came.

After the East African embassy bombings, US pressure on the Saudis increased. Prince Turki visited Kandahar to persuade Taliban to expel Osama bin Laden from Afghanistan. In their meeting Mullah Omar refused to do so and then insulted Prince Turki by abusing the Saudi royal family. Furious about the Taliban insults, the Saudis suspended diplomatic relations with the Taliban and ostensibly ceased all aid to them, although they did not withdraw recognition of the Taliban government.

By now bin Laden had developed considerable influence with the Taliban, but that had not always been the case. Taliban's contact with the Arab-Afghans and their pan-Islamic ideology was non-existent until the Taliban captured Kabul in 1996. Pakistan was closely involved in introducing bin Laden to the Taliban leaders in Kandahar, because it wanted to retain for Kashmiri militants the Khost training camps, which were now in Taliban hands. Increasingly bin Laden's worldview appeared to dominate the thinking of senior Taliaban leaders.

Initially the Taliban leadership was not particularly antagonistic to the USA or the West. In fact it was hoping for US recognition of the Taliban government. However under the influence of bin Laden and particularly after the East Africa bombings, Taliban began to be vocal in its criticism of the Americans, the UN, the Saudis and Muslim regimes around the world. Their utterances increasingly reflected the aggressive language of bin Laden and much different from their earlier style. As US pressure to expel bin Laden mounted, the Taliban said he was a guest and it was against Afghan tradition.

Ahmed Rashid observes:

> The Arab-Afghans had come full circle. From being mere

appendages to the Afghan jihad and the Cold War in the 1980s, they had taken centre stage for the Afghans, neighbouring countries and the West in the 1990s. The USA was now paying the price for ignoring Afghanistan between 1992 and 1996, when the Taliban were providing sanctuary to the most hostile and militant Islamic fundamentalist movement the world faced in the post-Cold War era. Afghanistan was now truly a haven for Islamic terrorism and the Americans and the West were at a loss as to how to handle it.[15]

Notes

1 Ahmed Rashid, *Taliban, the Story of the Afghan Warlords,* Pan Books, 2001. Originally published as *Taliban, Islam and Oil and the New Great Game in Central Asia,* L.B. Tauris, 2000.

2 Olivier Roy, *Afghanistan from Holy War to Civil War,* Princeton University Press, 1995.

3 Samuel P. Huntington, *The Clash of Civilization and the Remaking of the World Order,* Simon & Schuster, New York, 1996.

4 Ahmed Rashid, *Taliban, the Story of the Afghan Warlords.*

5 Ibid.

6 'Laden Planned a Global Islamic Revolution', AFP, August 27, 1995.

7 Ahmed Rashid, *Taliban, the Story of the Afghan Warlords.*

8 Martin Ewers, *Afghanistan: A New History,* Curzon 2001.

9 Rashid, *Taliban, Islam and Oil.*

10 Michael Dobbs, 'Kabul's Fall to End the Anarchy', *Washington Post,* September 29, 2001.

11 Rashid, *Taliban, the Story of the Afghan Warlords.*

12 Text of speech of November 18, 1996 received by several NGOs and journalists from US sources.

13 'Inside the Hunt for Osama', *Time,* December 21, 1998.

14 'Making a Symbol of Terror', *Newsweek,* March 1, 1999.

15 Rashid, *Taliban, the Story of the Afghan Warlords.*

5

The War Against Afghanistan

Afghanistan is famous for its carpets. A different kind of carpet, however, inaugurated President Bush's War on Terror in Afghanistan: a carpet of bombs.

Carpet-bombing is a technique that was first used by the Americans in Vietnam, meant to cause the maximum devastation in a specified area. In the initial stages of the attack against Afghanistan, senior US defence officials had claimed that such intensive bombing would not be required in Afghanistan. But as the war aims changed and widened, American strategies and tactics also underwent changes.

In his address to the nation on October 7, 2001, after the bombing of Afghanistan had begun, President Bush said, 'The name of today's military operation is "Enduring Freedom". We defend not only our precious freedom but also the freedom of people everywhere.' The aim of the war appeared to be quite specific then. President Bush informed the public that 'The US military has begun strikes against Al Qaeda terrorist training camps and military installations of the Taliban regime in Afghanistan. These carefully targeted actions are designed to disrupt the use of Afghanistan as a terrorist base of operation and to attack the military capability of the Taliban regime.' There was no mention, at this stage, of any intention to dislodge or oust the Taliban regime.

Yet, the War on Terror was actually a war on a hapless nation and its people. As William Pfaff wrote,

> What set out as an American war on terrorism has become a war against Afghanistan. The substitution of Afghanistan for terrorism, or the identification of the one with the other, is not only unjust but diverts US policy from where it was intended to go, to where it is the most simple to go. Afghanistan has been substituted for terrorism because Afghanistan is accessible to military power and terrorism is not. The employment of high-tech munitions against irrelevant targets is a distraction from measures that actually deal with the threat. Qaeda is not identical with terrorism. Nor is bin Laden himself, even though Washington has cast him as the personification of evil. . . . Bin Laden and his group are merely instances of [that] threat. If he is killed, he will be replaced. The causes of terrorism will remain, and they are political. Afghanistan and its people are no threat to the United States, but they are the ones taking the full weight of America's indignation.[1]

This indignation came in the shape of a high-tech war using some of the most sophisticated and biggest weapons available in the arsenal of the mightiest military power, against one of the smallest armies in the world. Defence Secretary Donald Rumsfeld stated that he could not rule out the possibility of using nuclear weapons in the war. In saying this, he was saying nothing new. The possible use of nuclear weapons is never ruled out in any war in which the United States takes part. The US did use the Daisy Cutter, the biggest bomb in its arsenal, in Afghanistan. Cluster bombs were dropped over vast areas. A few thousand food packets in the same orange colour as the cluster bombs were dropped so that the 'oppressed people of Afghanistan will know the generosity of America and its allies', as President Bush stated in his address.

The air attacks did not bring down the Taliban government; nor did the Northern Alliance's early attacks on Taliban positions. The American carpet of bombs had to be spread wide so that the Northern Alliance's forces could march to Kabul. They entered the city and took it over defying the specific instructions of the US and much to the consternation of Pakistan.

As early as October 22, 2001, reports of US bombing whole villages were surfacing. Human Rights Watch reported that the village of Chowkar Karez, 40 km north of Kandahar was bombed at night by US planes. According to that report, 'Many of the people in the village . . . ran out of their homes, afraid that the bombs would fall on the homes. All witnesses stated that the aircraft then returned to the area and began firing from guns.' First they were forced out in the open by the bombs, and as they came out, they were gunned down. When asked to respond to this report, the Pentagon spokesperson said on November 2, 'The people there are dead because we wanted them dead.'[2] The fact, however, is that those killed had nothing to do with the Taliban or Al Qaeda – the ruins of the levelled village revealed nothing of military value. As Sonali Kolhatkar, founder of 'Acting in Solidarity with Afghan People' (ASAP) wrote:

> This pattern continues with the one difference – Pentagon officials have taken to completely denying the existence of Afghan civilians. The British media recently published an eye witness report of the village of Kama Ado being destroyed by US bombs in which at least 40 people were killed. When asked to respond, a Pentagon spokesperson vehemently said it simply didn't happen. He said 'Nothing happened' – those were the exact words (*The Independent*). We are told 'nothing happened'

> when evidence of the war's real victims is presented. Afghan civilians do not even have the distinction of being called collateral damage anymore – they are now non-existent, simply standing in the way of our war.[3]

It is indisputable that the American air campaign in Afghanistan killed hundreds of civilians. This campaign was a high-tech one, based on a strategy that sought to minimize American casualties. This strategy produced a pattern of mistakes. On-site reviews over a six-month period threw up the following conclusions. In some cases, civilians died because they were targeted by mistake, or because in their eagerness to kill Al Qaeda and Taliban fighters, Americans did not carefully differentiate between civilians and military targets. In other cases, evidence suggests that many civilians were killed because air strikes hit precisely the targets they were aimed at. The Pentagon was relying on information from warlords and other Afghans whose loyalties were unclear in a country driven by decades of war and tribal rivalries. Often the information thus received was inaccurate or incomplete, or in some cases even deliberately misleading. The sum total of all this was that too often the Americans were attacking without adequately understanding what they were striking.

By middle of July 2002, for the first time, Afghan leaders were demanding a say in how air raids were being conducted. 'We have to be given a larger role', said the Afghan Foreign Minister Dr Abdullah. 'If things do not improve, well, I will certainly pray for the Americans and wish them success, but I will no longer be able to take part in this.'[4]

To many observers it appeared that the war against the Afghans was very much in line with the US's historical role in Afghanistan. In the 1970s, the US hired seven different political parties of fundamentalists called mujaheddin. These were extremists hired by the CIA during the Cold War to 'draw the Soviets into the Afghan trap' as later revealed by former National Security Adviser, Zbignew Brzezinsky. The CIA gave arms and ammunition to the mujaheddin – many of whom now comprise the Northern Alliance – worth billions of dollars, including American made Stinger missiles. Using these weapons and sophisticated training in the art of terror, these men successfully drove out the Soviets, but also waged a terrible war on their own people killing at least 45,000 people in Kabul alone in the civil war after the exit of the Soviet troops.

The official American myth is that 'everything changed' on the day four airliners were hijacked and used as bombs to kill nearly 3,000 people. The US military intervention in Afghanistan, by this account, was hastily improvized in less than a month. Deputy Defence Secretary Paul Wolfowitz, in a television interview on November 18, claimed that only three weeks went into planning the military onslaught.

Many military experts doubted this claim. For good reason too. Credible reports have appeared that the US was planning to take military action against Afghanistan and oust Taliban months before September 11. These reports include the prediction, made in July 2001, that 'if the military action went ahead, it would take place before the snows started falling in Afghanistan, by the middle of October at the latest.' The Bush administration began its bombing strikes on the hapless, poverty-stricken country on October 7, and ground attacks by US special forces began on October 19.

Throughout 1999, US pressure on Afghanistan had increased. On February 3 of that year, Assistant Secretary of State Karl E. Inderfurth and State Department Coordinator for Counter-terrorism Richard Clarke travelled to Islamabad, Pakistan, to meet the Taliban's Deputy Foreign Minister, Abdul Jalil. They warned him that the US would hold the government of Afghanistan responsible for any further terrorist attacks by bin Laden. Later in the year, the Clinton Administration and the then Prime Minister of Pakistan, Nawaz Sharif, agreed on a joint covert operation to kill Osama bin Laden.[5] The Pakistani commando team was ready to strike by October 1999, when Sharif was overthrown in a military coup by General Pervez Musharraf, who halted the proposed covert operation. The Clinton administration had to settle for a UN Security Council resolution that demanded that Taliban turn over bin Laden to 'appropriate authorities', but did not require he be handed over to the US.

According to a front-page article in the *Washington Post* on November 18, 2001, by Bob Woodward, the CIA had been mounting paramilitary operations in southern Afghanistan since 1997. Woodward provides details about the CIA's role in the current military conflict, which includes the deployment of a secret paramilitary unit, the Special Activities Division. This force began combat on September 27, using both operatives on the ground and Predator surveillance drones equipped with missiles that could be launched by remote control. Woodward says, 'For the last 18 months, the CIA has been working with tribes and warlords in southern Afghanistan, and the division's units have helped create a significant new network in the region of the Taliban's greatest strength'. This means the US spy agency was engaged in attacks against the Afghan regime from the spring of 2000, more than a year before September 11.

With the installation of George Bush in the White House, the focus of American policy in Afghanistan shifted from a limited incursion to kill or capture bin Laden to preparing military action intended to oust the Taliban regime. The British-based *Jane's International Security* reported on March 15, 2001 that the new

American administration was working with India, Iran and Russia 'in a concerted front against Afghanistan's Taliban regime.' On June 26, 2001, the journal *IndiaReacts* reported more details about this:

> India and Iran will 'facilitate' US and Russian plans for 'limited military action' against the Taliban if the contemplated tough new economic sanctions don't bend Afghanistan's fundamentalist regime. Diplomats say that the anti-Taliban move followed a meeting between US Secretary of State Colin Powell and Russian Foreign Minister Igor Ivanov and later between Powell and Indian Foreign Minister Jaswant Singh in Washington. . . . Russia, Iran and India have also held a series of discussions and more diplomatic activity is expected.

In the immediate aftermath of September 11, two reports appeared in the British media indicating that the US government had threatened military action against Afghanistan several months before September 11. The BBC's George Arney reported September 18, 2001 that American officials had told former Pakistan Foreign Secretary Niaz Naik in mid-July of plans for military action against the Taliban regime.

> Mr Naik said US officials told him at a meeting of the UN on Afghanistan that unless bin Laden was handed over swiftly, America would take military action to kill or capture both bin Laden and the Taliban leader, Mullah Omar. . . . The wider objective according to Mr Naik, would be to topple the Taliban regime and install a transitional government of moderate Afghans in its place – possibly under the leadership of the former Afghan king Zahir Shah.[6]

Four days later, on September 22, *The Guardian* confirmed

this account. The warnings to Afghanistan came out of a four-day meeting of senior US, Russian, Iranian and Pakistani officials at a hotel in Berlin in mid-July, the third in a series of back-channel conferences dubbed 'brainstorming on Afghanistan'. *The Guardian* made this important observation:

> The threats of war unless the Taliban surrendered Osama bin Laden were passed to the regime in Afghanistan by the Pakistani government, senior diplomatic sources revealed yesterday. The Taliban refused to comply but the serious nature of what they were told raises the possibility that bin Laden, far from launching the attacks on the World Trade Centre in New York and the Pentagon out of the blue 10 days ago, was launching a pre-emptive strike in response to what he saw as US threats.

This account of the preparations for war against Afghanistan brings us to September 11 itself. The terrorist attack that destroyed the WTC and damaged the Pentagon was an important link in the chain of causality that produced the US attack on Afghanistan. The US government had planned the war well in advance, but the shock of September 11 made it politically feasible, by stupefying public opinion at home and giving Washington essential leverage on reluctant allies abroad.

The goals and strategy of Operation Enduring Freedom underwent several revisions during the course of the war – actually during the first three weeks. The turbulence reflected the difficulty of finding a strategy that could reconcile the US Administration's immediate war aims with a set of broader, longer-term strategic considerations – such as stability in Afghanistan and in the region surrounding it.

More controversial and demanding were the possible goals regarding the Taliban. In the weeks leading up to the war, the

Bush administration exhibited an artful ambiguity about the goals and nature of the prospective military operation in Afghanistan. This was part of a calculated attempt to maximize the support of as many nations as possible in the war on terror and build a grand coalition. After the bombing began it was clear that the administration had moved from the earlier stated goal of punishing Taliban (in a limited way) for their association with bin Laden and coerce their co-operation in bringing him to justice, to the goal of toppling the Taliban, both as a form of punishment and in order to open the way for a new government in Afghanistan that would fully co-operate with US action not only in Afghanistan but in the region. The European allies, especially Britain, were taken into confidence on the second goal but governments like those of Pakistan were kept in the dark. When the President of Pakistan spoke to the nation pledging support to the US it was clear that he did not anticipate the removal of Taliban from power. The first to announce publicly the plan to oust Taliban was Tony Blair, the British Prime Minister.

During the operation's first month aerial bombardment proved more successful in rattling America's partners and alienating world opinion than in coercing or collapsing the Taliban. Besides directly claiming hundreds of civilian lives by early November, the bombing campaign exacerbated an already severe refugee problem and disrupted relief efforts, leading humanitarian agencies to call for a halt or pause. Joining this chorus were Pakistani President Musharraf, UN High Commissioner for Human Rights Mary Robinson and ex-king Zahir Shah. Reinforcing the impression of a bombing campaign gone awry were the destruction of a UN de-mining facility, the double bombing of a Red Cross food distribution centre, the destruction of a military hospital and accidental attacks on an old age home and boys' school. Several small villages and residential areas suffered severe attacks.

The American use of cluster bombs, which began in earnest during the last week of October, also drew sharp criticism from human rights and disarmament groups. In some cases cluster bombs had been used near civilian areas leaving ammunitions scattered among residences. Unexploded bomblets were found over a large area. The concern about cluster bombs was heightened by the fact that their submunitions were the same colour and approximate size of the food packets dropped by the US Air Force.

A shift in strategy unleashed the dogs of war and exposed the contradictions in objectives. The bombing campaign had been intensified during the second week – daily sorties rose from about 25 to 90 – after the Taliban had proved more resilient than initially expected and the Northern Alliance had failed in its initial effort to take Mazar-i-Sharif. But this was still consistent with hopes that the Taliban might be split and a part co-opted. The truly significant shift was the decision to cast America's lot with the Northern Alliance's military effort. In the Northern Alliance's troops the US air power found its required ground fulcrum. But it was a devil's bargain that cost America leverage and control on the strategic level. The contradiction inherent in fully supporting the Northern Alliance military effort was two-fold.

First, the Alliance's goals – beyond defeating the Taliban – were not the same as America's. Second, American leverage over the Northern Alliance would decrease as Alliance troops closed in on the victory that the US air power made possible. Thus fully supporting the Alliance meant losing control over it. The Alliance, fully aware of these facts, quickly discarded their promise of restraint once it became possible for them to ride into Kabul (and into power) without further American assistance.

The Alliance victory and Taliban collapse profoundly altered the national and regional strategic situation in several ways – none of them auspicious in terms of long-term stability.

First, the rapid victory of the Alliance and collapse of the Taliban released centrifugal tendencies throughout Afghanistan, giving war-lordism, banditry and opium production a new lease of life. This essentially erased the one positive feature of the Taliban period. An immediate effect was the aggravation of the country's humanitarian crisis. A longer-term effect would be greater difficulty in building a unified polity and resilient civilian authority.

Second, the advance of the Northern Alliance and defeat of the Taliban altered the principal lines of opposition in Afghan society. Rather than following a 'Taliban versus anti-Taliban' axis, the conflict was reoriented along purely ethnic, tribal and sect lines. This was likely to lead to a new bipolar configuration in the country, Pashtun versus non-Pashtun. The ethnic reframing of the Afghan struggle altered the political implications of US military operations in the country, which had focused almost exclusively on Pashtun areas since late-November.

Third, the increased salience of ethnic, tribal and sect lines of division also increased the centrifugal pressures on the international coalition supporting the coalition. Notably, the Alliance victory had substantially increased Russian influence in Afghanistan, contrary to US interests and to the dismay of both Pakistan and Iran. Indian interests (tied to the Tajik militias) also advanced substantially. These developments increased the prospects for intensified regional contention over Afghanistan. These outcomes were largely the result of the US having augmented and unleashed the Northern Alliance – a force over which it had insufficient control. The policy shift indicated the extent to which military expediency had come to dominate US strategic calculation.[7]

The potential for instability in post-Taliban Afghanistan resides in three systemic features of the new strategic environment. First, the present distribution of national and provincial authority in Afghanistan bears little relationship to the balance of interests and resources within and around the country. Instead it is a 'collateral effect or by-product' of Operation Enduring Freedom. Long-term local and regional players disfavoured by the war's outcome will mobilize resources and try to regroup and reassert. The post-Taliban balance between warlords and civilian authority decisively favours the former. No central or indigenous military authority yet comes close to exercising reliable or predominant control over the country, which remains a patchwork of fiefdoms and contested or lawless areas.

As Afghan and United Nations officials prepared for the *loya jirga* (grand national assembly) as called for in the 2001 Bonn agreement to choose Afghanistan's next government, ordinary Afghans were increasingly terrorized by the rule of local and regional military commanders – warlords – who are reasserting their control over large areas of Afghanistan, reported Human Rights Watch after a mission to southern Afghanistan in late May 2002. The mission uncovered credible evidence of the re-emergence of figures associated with the Taliban as well as the extremist Islamic movement led by former Afghan Prime Minister Gulbuddin Hekmatyar in several southern provinces. These warlords have been able to consolidate power because of the vacuum created when the US-led military coalition and the UN Security Council refused to expand the International Security Assistance Force (ISAF) beyond Kabul. Regardless of their ideology and the source of their support these warlords are creating a climate of repression that once again threatens the security and well being of the Afghan people. The US and its coalition forces have an active presence in southern Afghanistan and have used local troops supplied by warlords in combat operations. These activities have fostered the impression that the US is supporting the warlords, directly or indirectly.[8]

The clearest achievement of Operation Enduring Freedom was forcing the Taliban from power. But this goal was secondary to the one of destroying the Al Qaeda network – an aim that has been only partially achieved.

In the middle of June 2002 the commander of American troops in Afghanistan, Lt. General McNeill, said it would probably take at least one more year to fulfil his mission to crush the remnants of Al Qaeda and the Taliban forces in the country and build the foundations of an Afghan national army. He said that until those milestones were reached it was unlikely that the US or its allies would significantly reduce their forces in Afghanistan. 'Job one is close with and destroy those who would destroy us', McNeill said. 'Nation building is not in my charter.'[9] He was right, of course – nation building has never been in the American charter in its numerous military campaigns across the planet.

The extended presence of American and coalition forces could stir some resentment in the provinces, particularly near the Pakistan border and around Kandahar where the Taliban had strong support and where some local leaders have accused coalition forces of killing or detaining innocent civilians. The Pentagon is aware of those potential restraints and for that reason has consistently argued that the US has no intention of establishing permanent military bases in Afghanistan.

Many military analysts have described the current strategy for hunting Al Qaeda as counterinsurgency. The hunt is being carried out largely by small units of special operations forces working with Afghan soldiers, many of them affiliated with local warlords. As one commentator put it, 'It would be risky to assume either that Al Qaeda and the Taliban feel they have been defeated or that they do not still relish the chance to fight the Americans. The view from the terrorist side may be far more optimistic than we are led to believe by our government.'[10] 'The situation is quite like Vietnam', said Andrew Krepinevich, Executive Director of the Centre for Strategic and Budgetary Assessments, a military research group in Washington. 'As long as the regime in Kabul is perceived as weak, Taliban and other groups aligned with radical Islam will see the war as winnable and will continue to soldier on'. Even those who reject the historical parallels admit that the conflict has evolved from conventional to unconventional warfare in part at least due to the failure of the former.

Within Afghanistan itself Al Qaeda may well be relishing a victory over US and allied special forces in the battle of Sha-i-Kot near Gardez. This was the US operation that filled the TV screens in early March 2002. It was promoted as an assault that would surround and crush the Al Qaeda in the mountains. By the end of the battle many observers concluded that most of the Al Qaeda fighters escaped and the operation, far from being the 'unqualified success' the coalition forces claimed, was in fact a kind of victory for Al Qaeda. Dan Plesch warned that 'Like the Soviets before them, the US may find that its first year in Afghanistan is the best.'[11]

For the Karzai administration the mysterious escape of Osama bin Laden and Mullah Omar has turned out to be a curse as well as a blessing. On the one hand, the administration cannot breathe easy as long as they and their band of faithful men remain elusive. On the other, it provides a valid excuse for the US-led coalition to prolong its presence in Afghanistan.

As the war on Afghanistan continued, more and more information kept coming out about civilian casualties and atrocities by American troops. It is estimated that about 5,000 civilians have been killed. A documentary film, *Massacre in Mazar*, by the Irish director Jamie Doran was shown to selected audiences in Europe in June 2002, provoking demands for an international inquiry into US war crimes in Afghanistan. The film alleges that

American troops collaborated in the torture of POWs and the killing of thousands of captured soldiers near the town of Mazar-i-Sharif. It documents events following the November 21, 2001 fall of Konduz, Taliban's last stronghold in northern Afghanistan. Leading international human rights lawyer Andrew McEntee, who saw the film, said, 'it was clear there is a prima facie evidence of serious war crimes committed not just under international law but also under the law of the United States itself'. The Pentagon issued a statement on June 13 denying allegations of US complicity in the torture and murder of POWs and the US State Department followed suit with a formal denial on June 14.[12]

Selig Harrison, director of the Asia Programme at the Centre for International Policy and an authority on Afghan affairs wrote on the emerging situation in Afghanistan:

> The Pashtun goodwill earned by the United States for sweeping away the Taliban had been replaced by resentment after US pressure to block the re-emergence of a Pashtun-dominated regime at the recent 'loya jirga' or grand council, held in Kabul.
>
> When it hastily launched Operation Enduring Freedom last October, the United States cast its lot with a triumvirate of generals from the Tajik ethnic minority who helped to dislodge the Taliban and now dominate the government of Hamid Karzai, a largely powerless front man. This Tajik Triumvirate controls not only the armed forces and police, but also three hated secret police agencies. In Pashtun eyes, the secret police are dedicated to curbing Pashtun influence and were automatically suspect in last week's murder of Vice President Haji Abdul Qadir, although there is no evidence yet to support this suspicion.[13]

Some say that many factors caused severe conflict between Qadir, one of the US's most trusted allies in the eastern provinces, and the leaders of the Northern Alliance. In his death the US was deprived of an influential ally.

To counter Tajik control of the security apparatus and also Karzai's cabinet, Pashtun leaders wanted Zahir Shah to run for president of the New Transitional Authority at the *loya jirga*. He was to have critical but clearly limited powers, with Karzai as prime minister running the government. Selig S. Harrison wrote,

> On the eve of the 'loya jirga', the White House special envoy in Kabul, Zalmay Khalizad, openly demanded that Zahir Shah renounce his presidential candidacy to avoid a 'divisive' situation. Khalilzad confronted the king in a well-publicized meeting that one of the royal advisers described to me as 'unpleasant'.
>
> Khalizad is now reviled as 'the viceroy' by many Pashtuns, who refer to the once welcomed US forces in Afghanistan as an 'army of occupation'.[14]

'With sporadic fighting continuing across parts of Afghanistan instability remains a priority concern in the country', Lakhdar Brahimi, UN Secretary General's Special Representative reported to the Security Council on October 30, 2002. The envoy blamed ongoing human rights violations in Afghanistan on 'the weakness of the central government, warlordism, persistent factional conflicts in some parts of the country and a very basic and dysfunctional justice system'. He also pointed out that abuses against Pashtuns contribute a problem which threatens to have an adverse impact on the peace process. About 50,000 to 60,000 ethnic Pashtuns living in squalid camps in southern Afghanistan have refused to return to their homes in the north out of fear they will be discriminated against by ethnic Tajiks and Uzbeks who dominate the region. When Brahimi reported to the Security

Council on January 31, 2003, he said that while impressive gains hade been made over the past year, the country still faced tough challenges and the peace process was 'far from secure' amid worrying reports that support for the remnants of Taliban regime might be growing in some areas. So the overall peace process in Afghanistan needed to progress 'much further before we can safely say it is irreversible'. A spokesman for the United Nations, Manoel de Almeida e Silva said on 27 February that Afghanistan 'is in precarious state'. He told a news conference the UN has suspended aid work in parts of northern and southern Afghanistan because of fighting between rival factions and uncertain security conditions.

The authority of the Karzai government is limited largely to Kabul and its immediate environs and is absent in most of the rest of the country. Outside Kabul, the country is controlled by a myriad of major and minor warlords who carved out mini fiefdoms in the political vacuum that emerged following the fall of the Taliban. The central government lacks the wherewithal to subordinate these destabilising figures and will be unable to do so in the near future. Several of these warlords are supported by the US. Rudd Lubbers, the UN High Commissioner for Refugees had negotiations with three warlords including Abdul Rashid Dostum on 28 February 2003 regarding return of refugees. It was a recognition of both the limits of the central authority and the power wielded by the warlords.

The observation made by Mark Sedia in mid-November 2002 rings more true at the end of March 2003: 'The historical parallels between the present security situation and that which existed immediately prior to the Taliban's accent to power are striking and should not be overlooked. Security conditions in certain regional centres appear to have reverted to the *status quo ante* of 1992.'[15]

Notes

[1] William Pfaff, *International Herald Tribune*, November 3, 2001.
[2] *The New York Times,* November 3, 2001.
[3] *Commondreams,* December 12, 2001. *The New York Times* published a report on July 20, 2002 that proclaimed: 'Flaws in US Air War Left Hundreds of Civilians Dead'.
[4] *The New York Times,* July 20, 2002.
[5] As reported in *Washington Post*, October 3, 2001.
[6] *BBC News,* September 18, 2001.
[7] Project on Defence Alternatives Research Monograph, *Strange Victory: A critical appraisal of Operation Enduring Freedom and the Afghanistan War*, 30 January 2002.
[8] Human Rights Watch Briefing Paper, 'Afghanistan – Return of the Warlords'.
[9] *International Herald Tribune*, June 19, 2002.
[10] Dan Plesch, *Sunday Observer*, June 23, 2002.
[11] Ibid.
[12] *Asia Times*, June 14, 2002.
[13] Selig S. Harrison, *International Herald Tribune*, July 10, 2002.
[14] Ibid.
[15] Mark Sedia, *Foreign Policy in Focus*, November 15, 2002.

6

Violations of International Law

The bombing of Afghanistan inaugurated the War on Terror. A number of issues of international law are involved in this campaign, issues that have resurfaced with even greater focus and urgency in the war on Iraq. Was the US action a legitimate form of self-defence, as the Bush administration has repeatedly claimed? Was there an alternative to military action? What was the role of the United Nations? What are the implications of the War on Terror for human rights?

Right at the outset, we need to note that the US has a dismal record with regard to compliance with international laws. It's decade-long bombing campaign against Iraq is illegal. The bombing of Yugoslavia in 1999 had no sanction under international law. The US does not recognize the jurisdiction of the World Court. It withdrew from the Court in 1986 when the Court condemned Washington for attacking Nicaragua, mining its harbours and funding the Contras. In that case, the Court rejected the claim of the US that it was acting under Article 51 (of the UN Charter) in defence of Nicaragua's neighbours.

The first question that arises is whether the attacks on the World Trade Centre towers and the Pentagon constituted acts of war. From September 11 onwards the US has considered itself to be the victim of an act of war. This position received support from NATO, which activated Article 5 of its Charter committing 'member states to assist if any member state has been subjected to an armed attack'. According to Jordan Paust, Law Foundation Professor of the University of Houston,

> Under international law we [the US] could not be at 'war' with an entity that has a status less than that of an insurgent (which status pertains during an insurgency or armed conflict not of an international character within the meaning of Common Article 3 of the 1949 Geneva Conventions) unless that entity is directly involved with others engaged in a 'war'. We could not be at 'war' with Osama bin Laden, since he and his entourage are in no way representatives or leaders of an 'insurgency' within the meaning of international law. He is also not a recognized leader of a 'nation', 'belligerent' or 'state'.[1]

Most of the laws of war embodied in the 1949 Geneva Conventions and Protocols thereto are concerned with inter-state armed conflicts. Among the four Conventions, only Common Article 3 expressly applies to armed conflicts which are not inter-state. However that Article essentially contemplates internal armed conflict, the conflict occurring within the territory of one state. In the September 11 case there is neither inter-state conflict nor internal armed conflict, but a group or groups of non-state actors who are likely based abroad, possibly in several countries launching an attack against a state. It does not fit the model that international law provides. War in international law means armed conflict between nations. The terror attacks do not involve a war according to international law. It is not proven that the attacks can be ascribed to a state, a prerequisite for the war definition.

Issues of state responsibility and individual criminal responsibility under international law have also arisen with regard to the events of September 11. Indeed it is the link (or lack thereof) between these two types of responsibility that makes this case particularly complex. If the perpetrators were state agents sent by their governments to carry out these attacks, then calling this an 'act of war' and holding that government responsible would be fully justifiable. However as these acts were committed by non-state actors we are entering under-explored legal territory.

The stated position of the US that it makes 'no distinction between the terrorists who committed these acts and those who harbour them' also raises questions. While the phrase 'those who harbour them' is open to a variety of interpretations, it was apparently intended to refer to states that harbour terrorists. There are different ways in which the responsibility of a state can arise with respect to the acts of non-state actors. According to the Draft Articles of State Responsibility of the International Court of Justice, 'The conduct of a person or group of persons shall be considered an act of a State under international law if the person or group of persons is in fact acting on the instructions of or under the direction or control of the State in carrying out the conduct'.[2] The threshold for holding states accountable for the failure to prevent violations by non-state actors has to be considerably lowered or even abandoned to hold Afghanistan accountable for the acts of September 11.

The UN Security Council is on record of having rejected claims to right of self-defence as justification of armed attack against 'states harbouring terrorists'. On October 1, 1985 Israeli planes bombed the headquarters of the Palestine Liberation Organisation at Hammam-Plage, near Tunis, Tunisia. In explaining its action to the Security Council, Israel argued that the bombing was justified since Tunisia knowingly harboured terrorists who had targeted Israel. The Security Council rejected the claim of Israel and voted in Resolution 573 to condemn the Israeli action by a margin of 14-0 with the United States abstaining. It is important to note that the US *did not veto the resolution*. The resolution condemned 'vigorously the act of armed aggression perpetrated by Israel against Tunisian territory in flagrant violation of the Charter of the United Nations, international law and norms of conduct'. It described the air raid as 'a threat to peace and security in the Mediterranean region'. The resolution further requested UN member states 'to take measures to dissuade Israel from resorting to such acts against the sovereignty and integrity of all States'.[3]

Despite repeated references to Article 51 of the UN Charter, the United States cannot claim justification for attack on Afghanistan under the provisions of that Article. The Article states, 'Nothing in the present Charter shall impair the inherent right of individual or collective self-defence if an armed attack occurs against a Member of the United Nations, until the Security Council has taken measures necessary to maintain international peace and security'. The right ceases at the point when the Security Council begins its action. In this case the Security Council had immediately begun to take action.

The Security Council passed two unanimous resolutions on terrorist attacks on the US. It adopted Resolution 1368 on September 12 that unequivocally condemned the terrorist attacks on the US and called on the international community to redouble its efforts to prevent and suppress terrorist acts. On September 28 it passed the more specific and far-reaching Resolution 1373. In this resolution it acted under Chapter VII of the UN Charter, which gave the Security Council authority to order states to carry out the measures decided upon by the Security Council. It reiterated that terrorist acts constitute a threat to international peace and security. It also announced a series of measures for the legal suppression of terrorism and for co-operation between states in security, intelligence, criminal investigation and proceedings related to terrorism. The Security Council set up a Committee to monitor progress on the measures in the resolutions and asked all states to report back to it.

Resolution 1373 concludes with an expression of the Security Council's determination to 'take all necessary steps' to ensure its full implementation. The quoted words are reminiscent of the Council's authorization to member states in Resolution 678 to 'use all necessary means' to restore international peace and security after Iraq invaded Kuwait in 1990. But significantly Resolution 1373 does not 'authorize states' to 'take all necessary steps' to implement it. Instead it determines that the Council itself stands ready to take steps, which presumably could involve an authorization of some form of armed force to ensure that the measures taken in the resolution were adequately implemented. Such an authorization was not made. The Security Council resolution of September 12 recognized a threat to world peace but not an armed attack, which alone could trigger the right to self-defence. The resolution of September 28 also identifies the threat to peace but not an armed attack. The significance of this text is that it emphasizes non-military sanctions and refrains from belligerent measures.[4]

Both resolutions in their preambles abstractly 'affirm' the inherent right of individual or collective self-defence as recognized by the Charter. This, however, cannot be construed as a Security Council approval of the use of armed force as a response to the events of September 11. They do not say or mean that military action against Afghanistan would be within the right of self-defence.

> A country is not permitted to use military force for purposes of retaliation, vengeance or punishment. In other words, unless a future attack on the United States is imminent, it cannot use

> military force. This means that even if the United States furnishes evidence as to the authors of the September 11 attack, it cannot use military force against them. To this extent the Congressional resolution authorizing the President to use force against the perpetrators of the attack on September 11 is a violation of international law. Instead, the US must employ other means including extradition and resolution of the Security Council, which could eventually authorize the use of force to effectuate the arrests of suspects.[5]

Article 2 of the Charter prohibits the use or threatened use of force against another state. The Article 2 prohibition is a rule of customary international law and is universally binding. This has been reiterated in numerous resolutions of the UN General Assembly. For example on December 17, 1984, the UN General Assembly passed a resolution containing the demand 'that all states take no action aimed at military intervention and occupation, forcible change in or undermining the socio-political system of States, destabilization and overthrow of their governments and in particular, initiate no military action to that end under any pretext whatsoever and cease forthwith any such action already in progress'.

Therefore it is evident that the military action by the US and its allies against Afghanistan is not within the ambit of the UN resolutions or in accordance with the Charter. The Secretary General of the UN stated on October 8, 2001, that 'the States carrying out their military action in Afghanistan have set it in the context of the determination expressed by the Security Council immediately after the September 11 attacks to use all means to combat threats to international peace and security caused by terror acts'. He seemed to be following a fashion in the UN since 1991 for post-facto legitimization of US-led military actions. What is to be noted specially is that the Security Council, which met on October 8 and heard a briefing on the military action that was launched on the previous day, did not take any action. There was no endorsement from the Council like the one given by the Secretary General. The Council President only said that the US and the British delegates had told the Council that action had been taken in self-defence against those who were responsible for the attack and those who harboured them. That claim was belied not only by the magnitude and scale of the attacks in the following days but by a statement in the letter from the US Ambassador to the President of Security Council regarding the action.

In his letter Ambassador Negroponte described the September 11 terrorist acts as 'armed attacks carried out against the US'. He said, 'There is still much we do not know. Our enquiry is still in its early stages'. Then he added ominously, 'We may find that our self-defence requires further action with respect to other organizations and other states'. This was anticipatory justification of the illegal military action against Iraq, which started in March 2003, as well as future such actions against other states in different parts of the world. The letter was an open defiance of the UN Charter. It implied that the US was ready to launch attacks against any state. It did not need any authorization or permission for its attack on Afghanistan. It would act unilaterally. Even though the evidence was admittedly scanty and the enquiry was still in the early stages it was ready to go to war. Secretary General Kofi Annan stated that he and his colleagues were 'disturbed' by the statement. What he should have pointed out was that the admitted vagueness and lack of adequate information about those responsible for the 'armed attacks against the US', negated the claim of self-defence in the military action against Afghanistan. What the US was claiming through the letter of the Ambassador was not the right of self-defence but a 'right' for pre-emptive attacks against any state. This was a declaration that the US would blatantly violate international law.

Already in September 2001 many legal experts suggested an alternative to the use of military force. For instance,

> The Security Council can establish an international tribunal to try those suspected of involvement in the September 11 attacks as it did with regard to Rwanda and the former Yugoslavia and request the extradition of suspects. It could apply sanctions to countries that refuse to comply as it did successfully against Libya – a strategy that resulted in the trials in The Hague according to the laws of Scotland. It can establish a UN force to effectuate arrests, prevent attacks or counter aggression (Articles 41–50). Measures the Security Council can employ include interruptions of economic relations, rail, sea, air, postal, telegraphic, radio communications and severance of diplomatic relations.[6]

But for the alternate route evidence that would satisfy an international tribunal was needed against those who were accused by the United States of having perpetrated the crime.

A document was presented to the British Parliament on October 4 by Prime Minister Tony Blair claiming it contained evidence that Osama bin Laden and the Al Qaeda network planned and carried out the September 11 hijack-bombings in New York and Washington. A few days earlier Washington had reneged on a promise made by Secretary of State Colin Powell to make public the evidence it claimed to possess of bin Laden's guilt. The document presented by Blair was part of an international effort to placate America's wavering allies against the background of demand for proof in many countries.

The dossier begins with the following caveat: 'This document does not purport to provide a prosecutable case against

Osama bin Laden in a court of law'. This acknowledgement is rationalized on the grounds that 'Intelligence often cannot be used evidentially, due both to the strict rules of admissibility and to the need to protect the safety of sources'. This has serious implications. The premise that a lower standard of evidence is sufficient to justify a war than would be the norm for establishing innocence or guilt in a court of law is, at best, dubious. The incalculable consequences of a military attack argue for a standard of proof no less strict than that required in a legal case. In court what is at stake is the fate of defendants as individuals, whereas Britain and the US were about to launch a military campaign in which the lives of an unknown number of innocent civilians were threatened. According to the claim in the document, the 'need to protect the safety of sources' was greater than the lives of thousands of people in Afghanistan. The claim that intelligence consideration prohibit those about to wage war from presenting evidence justifying such a course was a blanket rationalization for any and all military action. In fact the British government's document was not a serious presentation of evidence, and fell short of the rigorous standards of a legal requirement. It was devoid of any independently verifiable facts that establish the guilt of bin Laden, Al Qaeda or the Taliban in connection with the September 11 terror attacks.[7]

Most of what the document put forward had been previously reported in the media. All of its allegations were unsubstantiated. The document is divided into three main headings. The most crucial is the section purporting to deal with Al Qeada's role in the September 11 terror attacks. This constitutes just nine points out of the seventy contained in the 15-page dossier. In an evident attempt to obscure the flimsy character of this pivotal section, the authors have filled the bulk of the document with pages purportedly outlining Al Qaeda's previous involvement in terrorist attacks against the US, together with a presentation of the historical origins of bin Laden's Al Qaeda network and the Taliban regime.

In the section dealing with September 11, only one apparently concrete connection between Al Qaeda and the hijack-bombings is made: the claim that of the 19 identified hijackers, 'At least three of them have already been positively identified as associates of Al Qaeda. One has been identified as playing key roles in both the East African embassy attacks and the USS Cole attack.' But this statement raises more questions than it answers. If the identities of the three are known, why are they not named? The comment by Jamal Khashoggi, Deputy Editor-in-Chief, Arab News, is pertinent in this connection:

> Here in Saudi Arabia people are grasping at inaccuracies in the evidence presented by the FBI. In the early days of the investigation one of the accused Saudis was found to have been dead for a year before the attack. Another was arrested and then released. Five others were found to be living with their families. Even though the FBI has now revised the list of accused hijackers, the doubts have been cast and now conspiracy theories abound.[8]

Regarding the events of September 11, the document goes on to make further assertions: that bin Laden himself declared shortly before September 11 that he was preparing a major attack on America and called close associates to return to Afghanistan from other parts of the world by September 10, and that 'Since September 11 we have learned that one of bin Laden's closest and most senior associates was responsible for the detailed planning of the attacks'. Needless to say, this man is not named. Then follows the significant statement: 'There is evidence of a very specific nature relating to the guilt of bin Laden and his associates that is too sensitive to release'. Whether or not the authors of the document realize it, this sentence amounts to a tacit admission that they have produced nothing of a 'specific nature' proving a connection between bin Laden and the September 11 attacks.

Politically the most significant part of the British dossier is the section that purports to outline the historical origins of Al Qaeda and the Taliban regime. The document takes as its starting point the year 1989, when, it claims, bin Laden and others founded Al Qaeda. The authors conveniently omit any reference to the previous decade: the Soviet invasion and US support for the mujaheddin.

To point out, by exposing this document, that the US could not produce evidence against bin Laden that would stand the scrutiny of an international tribunal, is in no way to suggest that he was not responsible for the attack. While in all probability he was behind the attacks, it has to be pointed out that the document conveniently omits any mention of the real origins of Al Qaeda. The American CIA, with the assistance of the British Special Air Service (SAS), funded, trained and armed the mujaheddin as part of the Cold War struggle against the Soviet Union that militarily intervened in Afghanistan in 1979 and withdrew ten years later. As mentioned earlier, among those with whom the Americans worked to undermine Soviet influence was Osama bin Laden.

There can be only two possible explanations for this kind of 'evidence'. Either the US government has no proof of a direct connection between Osama bin Laden, the Taliban and the September 11 attacks, or it cannot release the evidence it has because the information would in some way implicate individuals or organizations connected to American intelligence or that of an allied state. It was clear from the outset that the US was not interested in pursuing a path under international law and instead wanted to take military action against Afghanistan as the beginning of its War on Terror.

There are very serious implications of the War on Terror for human rights.

According to the US-based Human Rights Watch (HRW), many governments around the world are using the US-led War on Terror as an excuse to carry out repressive polices and suppress internal dissent and opposition. Its report says that the US and its Western allies are turning a blind eye to human rights abuses in friendly countries in return for their support in the campaign against terror. HRW condemns the September 11 attack, calling it 'antithetical to the values of human rights'. It says that it was concerned that following the attacks many governments tend to take advantage of the situation by touting their own internal struggles as battles against terrorism.[9]

A striking example is Russia. Its President was one of the firsts to embrace anti-terrorism rhetoric. He succeeded in using it to defend the brutal campaign in the breakaway republic of Chechenya. Western countries downplayed their earlier criticism of Moscow's human rights abuses as they set about building a US-led coalition against international terror. In the days following September 11, German Chancellor Gerhard Schroder and Italian Prime Minister Slivio Berlusconi said that Russia's action in Chechenya must be reassessed. The US toned down its criticism of human rights abuse by Russia and played up alleged links between Chechen rebels and Osama bin Laden.

Two other countries, which are specifically mentioned by the HRW *Report* as having taken advantage of the war against terrorism for domestic oppression are Uzbekistan, which shares a border with Afghanistan, and Egypt. Uzbekistan is singled out as particularly repressive and an example of how the West can overlook torture and other abuses because of the country's strategic importance. The Egyptian government has brushed off criticism of torture and summary trials, suggesting that Western countries should 'think of Egypt's own fight against terror as their new model'. The West has quietly accepted this pattern of repression because in the short term it seems to promise stability and because the democratic alternative is feared. Egypt has secured from the US government massive aid and tacit acceptance of its human rights violations.

The most blatant example of the use of the war on terror for gross violation of human rights is the policy of Israel against the Palestinians. Prime Minister Ariel Sharon has repeatedly referred to Palestinian leader Yassir Arafat as 'our bin Laden' and claimed that his government's fight against the Palestinians was part of the War on Terror. The Palestinian authority is demolished, Palestinian territories are reoccupied and atrocities committed against the Palestinian people, all in the name of War on Terror. The US has fully supported the Israeli stance. The conceptual flaw in the War on Terror has become the biggest threat to the struggle of the Palestinian people for the right of self-determination.

The softening of the US government's attitude to human rights violations to friendly countries is reflected in the State Department's *Country Reports on Human Rights Violations*.[10] Support for the fight against terrorism is more important than concern for human rights. Typical is a passage commenting on military tribunals in Egypt. In 2001, the *Report* complained about the absence of due process. In 2002 after the US itself established such tribunals, the section concludes, 'Nonetheless judges have guidelines for sentencing, defendants have the right to counsel and statements of the charges against defendants are made public'. There are also indications of careful positioning over Uzbekistan, the former Soviet Republic north of Afghanistan, which became a crucial staging post for US operations. In the process of building up a 'civilized' coalition, the US has deepened its military ties with countries with records of human rights violations. The State Department *Report* foreshadows some of the problems with those relationships. In the State Department's entries for the new allies in the war on terrorism, the recurrent wording is 'the government's human rights record remained poor'.

'Can the goals of a tension-free world be achieved with such partners?' asks Frida Berrigan. 'To answer that question it is useful to look at the weapon sales and military training being offered to Bush administration's new partners in the war on terrorism alongside the State Department's recent report on their human rights records.'[11] The list includes Azerbaijan, Armenia, Georgia, Indonesia, Yemen, Colombia, Philippines and Uzbekistan. By lifting sanctions on arms transfers to countries with poor human rights records, as reward for their help in the war on terror, the US has 'degraded its human rights policy', says HRW in its *Report*. 'These transfers won't make the US more secure in the long run', said HRW Arms Division Director Joose Hilterman, 'and they make the US complicit in the abuse of civilians in other countries'.[12] The *Report* specially mentions the lifting in January 2002 of an eight-year-old ban on arms sales to Tajikistan that has 'a history of torture, suppression of political opposition and the media, and arrests based on religion'. The US also promised $43 million for security and for its cooperation in the war on terror despite 'its abysmal human rights record which includes torture and extensive religious persecutions'. And in Afghanistan, the *Report* said that the US has begun delivering weapons and ammunition to anti-Taliban forces with 'little effort to keep the equipment and ammunition out of the hands of the worst human rights abusers.'[13] Among the beneficiaries are many warlords, old and new.

In the US itself, in the name of the War on Terror, human

rights have been violated through new Executive Orders and arbitrary actions and constitution of military tribunals to try suspects, especially of foreign origin. The over-arching Patriot Act gives the government power to arrest suspects and detain them almost indefinitely, deport them, hold them in solitary confinement, open their mail, tap their phones, monitor their e-mail and search their homes without a warrant.

In an editorial, the *New York Times* said:

> The Bush administration's misguided effort to side-step America's existing civil and military courts to prosecute Al Qaeda and Taliban suspects in military tribunals has lurched from one problem to another. Now the Pentagon is coming with a legal theory that it will bring 200 detainees before the tribunals in the absence of specific evidence that they themselves have committed war crimes. This is a distressing exercise. In the US we do not arrest people and then devise laws to prosecute and convict them. Public confidence in the outcome of these trials demands a return to established American legal principles including independent court review.[14]

The Independent (London) reported 28 February that since September 11, up to 2,000 people have been detained in the US without trial or charge or legal rights. The fate of most is unknown. A *Washington Post* report said on March 12, that since September 11, the US government has secretly transported dozens of people suspected of links to terrorists in countries other than the US bypassing extradition procedure and legal formalities, according to Western diplomats and intelligence sources. The suspects have been taken to countries including Egypt and Jordan whose intelligence agencies have clear ties to CIA and where they can be subjected to interrogation tactics – including torture and threats to their families – that are illegal in the US, the sources said. In some cases US intelligence agents remain closely involved in the interrogation. The detention and treatment of Al Qaeda fighters in the US military base at Guantanamo Bay in Cuba, called Camp X-Ray, clearly violate international laws. Amnesty International says that the conditions there are cruel and inhuman with prisoners having no access to legal representation and accuses the US government of denying or threatening to deny internationally recognized rights of the suspects.

The American government's selective approach to the Geneva Conventions is legally unsustainable, as is its failure to respect fundamental human rights standards. The US has refused to grant any of those detained prisoner-of-war status or bring any disputed cases before a competent tribunal as required under the Geneva Conventions. Pentagon says the detainees are not prisoners of war protected by the Conventions and describes them as 'unlawful combatants'. If there is any doubt about their status, the Pentagon or its chief or any other administrative official has no authority to make such determination. According to Article 5 of the Third Geneva Convention, the US must allow a 'competent tribunal', which is impartial and independent, to determine the status of the prisoners.

Several countries have enacted laws that restrict and violate human rights, in the name of the War on Terror. A new draconian anti-terrorism law has been enacted in Britain without any proper parliamentary scrutiny. The Anti-Terrorism, Crime and Security Act which has the same aim as USA's Patriot Act permits indefinite detention without trial – internment by another name – on non-Britons whom the Home Secretary 'reasonably' believes are terrorists or have links with an international terrorist group or are 'a risk' to national security. 'Terrorism' is defined in the Act covering 'the use or threat of action' designed to influence the government or to advance a 'political, religious or ideological cause'. Such action includes the threat of committing 'serious damage to property'.[15]

To impose indefinite detention, the British government had to suspend its obligations under the European Convention on Human Rights and the UN's International Covenant on Civil and Political Rights. The 'derogation order' tabled by the Home Secretary meant the emergency was such that there was 'a threat to the life of the nation'. The order was made even though the security services reported that they did not have any evidence of specific threat to Britain. The *Sunday Observer of London* wrote on March 10, 2002: 'We do not lack legal powers to tackle terrorism – far from it. The new power is simply about imprisoning people where there is no quality evidence that they have committed any crime'.

The Prevention of Terrorism Ordinance (POTO, October 2001) and the Prevention of Terrorism Act (POTA, March 2002) in India have also to be seen as related to the War on Terror. While they can claim ancestry to an earlier law, the hasty manner in which the Ordinance was promulgated, its timing and the rationale given by the government link them to the global project of restricting human rights in the name of fighting terrorism. The government claimed that the law was in line with the US and British laws enacted after the September 11 terror attacks. Introducing the Bill to replace the Ordinance in Parliament, the Home Minister said that after the September 11 strikes in the US 'the democracies the world over have enacted far more stringent laws and it is not that they have abandoned human rights'. He added that the UN Security Council had also asked member states to enact laws against terrorism. The government argued that after September 11, terrorism has attained global dimensions and India is only complying with the Security Council Resolution 1373 of September 28 enjoining member states to undertake comprehensive measures to deal with terrorism. The Bush administration praised the Indian law. On March 28, 2002, the US State Department spokesman Richard Boucher declared in relation to the Indian Bill: 'It is important for the government to take steps against terrorism'.

What distinguishes the Indian law is that whereas the US and the UK laws are aimed mainly at non-citizens and aliens, POTA is aimed at India's own citizens. Yet the government goes on saying that terrorism in India comes from across the border. Many features of the Indian law are draconian. It does not contain a definition of 'terrorism', limiting itself to terrorist act. The definition is so vague and sweeping that anybody and everybody can be brought under its dragnet. Indeed, this is precisely what has happened, with more than one Chief Minister invoking the Act to book political rivals.

Some senior UN officials have begun to realize that Security Council Resolution 1373 of September 28 has been misused by some member states to justify repression of domestic dissent. Compliance with the Security Council requirements 'could lead to unwarranted infringement in civil rights', Bacre Waly Ndiaye, the chief human rights officer at UN Secretariat told the Council's new Counter-terrorism Committee. 'There is evidence that some countries are now introducing measures that may erode core human rights safeguards'. In an unexpectedly swift response to the attack on the WTC and the Pentagon, the Security Council had called on UN members on September 28 to provide information within ninety days about their legal restrictions on fund raising, financial transfers, arms acquisition and immigration. 'In some countries', Ndiaye told the Committee at its December 13, 2001, meeting, 'non-violent activities have been considered as terrorism and excessive measures have been taken to suppress or restrict individual rights including the presumption of innocence, the right to a fair trial, freedom from torture, privacy rights, freedom of expression and assembly and the right to seek asylum'.[16]

It is ironic that a resolution of the Security Council of the United Nations, established to reaffirm faith in fundamental human rights and for the promotion of equal rights of all, is misused by some member states to restrict and violate human rights. 'There is an erosion of civil liberties in the name of combating terrorism', Mary Robinson, UN High Commissioner for Human Rights said, in a speech to the Organization for Security and Cooperation in Europe. 'We are getting reports from human rights defenders, trade unionists, and journalists around the world that measures are being taken by countries saying that they're combating terrorism but in fact clamping down on political opposition, freedom of the press, branding activities as being terrorist which were not so described before 11th of September'.[17]

In this, as in much else, the United States has led by example.

Notes

1 Jordan Paust, 'War and Response to Terrorism', *ASIL (American Society of International Law) Insights*, September 2001.

2 John Cerone, 'Acts of War and State Responsibility in 'Muddy Waters' – The Non-State Actor Dilemma', *ASIL Insights*, September 2001. While the Draft articles are not binding law, they are largely in accord with the decisions of the ICJ and are highly persuasive evidence of the state of customary law.

3 UN Security Council Resolution 573, 1985.

4 Gerd Winter, *Taz*, October 2/3, 2001.

5 Michael Ratner, *Jurist*, available at www.jurist.law.pitt.edu/forumnew/32.htm.

6 Michael Ratner *Jurist Guest Column*, October 2001.

7 Chris Marsden and Barry Grey, 'Tony Blair bin Laden Dossier a Pretext instead of Proof', *World Socialist Website*, October 6, 2001.

8 Jamal Khashogi, *Arab View* 21-1-01.

9 *Annual Report*, Human Rights Watch, January 2002.

10 *Country Reports on Human Rights Violations*, US State Department, 2002.
11 Frida Berrigan, *Foreign Policy in Focus*, April 1, 2002.
12 AFP, Washington, February 14, 2002.
13 Ibid.
14 *The New York Times*, April 25, 2002.
15 Richard Norton Taylor, *The Guardian*, January 22, 2002.
16 William Orme, *Los Angeles Times*, January 2, 2002.
17 *Toronto Globe and Mail*, July 20, 2002.

7

Armies and Pipelines

> As the Roman Empire spread two millenniums ago, maps had to be redrawn to reflect new realities. In similar fashion the expansion of the British empire kept cartographers at their drawing boards, reshaping territories from Southern Africa to India to Hong Kong.
>
> Now as the United States wages its war on terrorism in Afghanistan – and deploys troops for the first time in the energy-rich regions of Central Asia and the Caucasus – the borders of a new American empire appear to be forming. Firmly in the Russian and later Soviet sphere of influence since Napoleon's day, these strategic regions, along with their Middle Eastern ramparts to the south, are now home to 60,000 American troops. Some of these soldiers are building what appear to be long-term bases at remote Central Asian outposts, raising critical questions about America's future role.[1]

Already 3,000 Americans are based in Uzbekistan and are believed to run both overt and covert operations in Afghanistan from there. US commanders are setting up new facilities in Krygyzstan for a combat air wing with 3,000 more troops. A deal has been struck with Tajikistan.

In short a constellation of air and army bases designed for long-

> term strategic control of the region is being installed under the command of the newly activated US 3rd army, whose headquarters was recently shifted from southern US to Kuwait. The so-called war on terrorism is being used to mask a far grander imperial design – the overthrow of Saddam Hussein that will allow the US to gain control of Iraq's huge oil reserves, which are second only to Saudi Arabia's. The new US bases just happen to follow the route of the planned pipelines that will bring Central Asia's oil and gas riches – the new Silk Road.[2]

The Washington Post said on February 29, 2002, that the base in Krygyzstan 'embodies what senior defence officials say is a major commitment to maintain not just air operation over Afghanistan for the foreseeable future but also a robust military presence in the region well after the war'. The *Post* said this military expansion in the Central Asian region has an added urgency to the US due to Saudi Arabian unease about American military presence on its soil:

> It is a sentiment that could force the United States to withdraw from the bases it first occupied in Saudi Arabia during the Persian Gulf War 11 years ago, leaving a potentially huge void in the military's ability to operate in the region. . . . The US administration is now giving armed forces the ability to conduct anti-terrorist operation on a near-permanent basis across much of the Muslim world. It is also establishing a broader political and security relationship with the Republics of Central Asia, a strategic region rich in oil and gas reserves.

In a testimony before the US Senate sub-committee hearing, Elizabeth Jones, Assistant Secretary of State for Eurasian Affairs said in December 2001 that the US would not abandon

Central Asia after the Afghan war. Jones outlined four US priorities in the region: combating terrorism, reform, the rule of law, and Caspian Sea energy resources. One may say that the first three are meant to ensure the fourth. 'We will not leave Central Asia after resolving the [Afghan] conflict. The stakes in Central Asia are undoubtedly high'.[3] Around the same time, US Secretary of State Colin Powell said that Kazakhstan's oil was becoming of 'critical importance'. With worldwide demand for oil increasing and the Gulf States – in particular Saudi Arabia – vulnerable to instability, the US is desperate to tap the vast untapped fields of Kazakhstan and other Central Asian states. There is thus an important subtext to the war on Afghanistan.

'Caspian reserves could be critical to future global energy supply', noted the respected London-based *Jane's Foreign Report* in March 2002. 'This is in line with the doctrine of "full-spectrum dominance" that now seems to govern American foreign policy and is manifesting itself in the Caucasus and Central Asia'. Indeed, many analysts pointed to the 'oil factor' as soon as the US began its Afghan military campaign. 'US influence and military presence in Afghanistan and the Central Asian states, not unlike that over the oil-rich Gulf states, would be a major strategic gain', said V.R. Raghavan, a strategic analyst and a former general of the Indian army. Raghavan commented that the prospect of a western military presence in the region extending from Turkey to Tajikstan could not have escaped strategists who were readying a military campaign aimed at changing the political order in Afghanistan.[4] The energy resources of the Caspian Sea and Central Asia were estimated between 100 and 150 billion barrels (bb) by the USA in the early 1990s. This figure was probably inflated and current estimates vary. But as Ahmed Rashid writes,

> Nevertheless, the Caspian represented possibly the last

> unexplored and unexploited oil bearing region in the world and its opening up generated huge excitement amongst international oil companies. . . . The scramble for oil and influence by the big powers in the Caspian has been likened to the Middle East in the 1920s. But Central Asia today is an even complex quagmire of competing interests. Big powers such as Russia, China and the USA, the neighbours Iran, Pakistan, Afghanistan and Turkey, the Central Asian states themselves, and the most powerful players of all, the oil companies, compete in what I called in 1997 . . . 'The New Great Game'.[5]

A 1997 *Backgrounder* of the right-wing think-tank Heritage Foundation said:

> Of the many foreign policy challenges the US faces during the post-Cold War era, one in particular is gaining importance with the passage of time: how best to secure adequate access to oil and natural gas in the first half of the 21st century. The oil and natural gas reserves of Eurasian and Caspian Sea region could provide the United States with a solution to this challenge. They are an abundant resource, second only to those in the unstable Middle East. The region's reserves of natural gas are similarly enormous – larger than those in all of North America. But the issue of access to the oil and natural gas of the region is not an isolated one, it is linked to other important US geo-strategic interests in Eurasia.[6]

The *Backgrounder* asked the US administration to recognize that the Caucasus and Central Asia ceased to be in the Russian sphere of influence with the collapse of the Soviet Union. It suggested that 'the US has many reasons to contribute to the revival of the region by participating in the development of an extensive network of pipelines, railroads, highways, ports, airports and telecommunications that can serve as a "Silk Road" to link the East and West in the Third Millennium'.

The US had been aggressively involved in the scramble for oil in the Middle East. When the popularly elected Mohammed Mossadeq threatened to nationalize Iranian oil in 1953, US and British secret services conspired in overthrowing him and restoring the Shah to power. The political rationale for this intervention was the 'communist threat'. So Cold War ideology became a convenient cover for what would become an oil bonanza for American and British petroleum companies.

Protection of oil interests in the region became a matter of over-riding concern to successive US administrations. The so-called Carter doctrine, based on President Carter's State of the Union address in 1980, in the aftermath of the Iranian revolution, made clear that an 'attempt by any outside force to gain control of the Persian Gulf will be regarded as an assault on the vital interests of the United States of America, and such an assault will be repelled by any means necessary, including military force'. It is no surprise, therefore, that when Saddam Hussein became a threat to America's oil interests, the (first) Gulf War was launched. According to Michael Klare, the danger to US oil rule is 'most acute in a vast triangular region stretching from the Persian Gulf in the West to the Caspian Sea in the north and the China Sea in the south. Within this "Strategic Triangle" can be found some of the world's largest concentrations of petroleum, along with numerous territorial disputes of powerful states'.[7]

In 1998, the California-based UNOCAL, which held 46.5 per cent stakes in Central Asia Gas (CentGas), a consortium that planned an ambitious gas pipeline across Afghanistan, withdrew in frustration after several fruitless years. The story of UNOCAL's pipeline enterprise in Afghanistan is highly relevant as it substantially influenced US policy towards the Taliban during the Clinton administration. UNOCAL's ambitious Central Asian Pipeline Project envisaged among its projects a 1,050-mile oil pipeline form Chardzhou in Turkmenistan to an oil terminal on Pakistan's coast. The Clinton administration's and UNOCAL's sudden interest in Turkmenistan and Afghanistan was not accidental. It was preceded by a significant change in US policy towards Central Asia with growing strategic interest displayed in a manner to challenge Russia. UNOCAL depended considerably on the US embassy in Islamabad and embassy facilities were used liberally for company-related meetings.

In July 1997 Strobe Talbot gave a speech that was to become the benchmark for US policy in the region. 'It has been fashionable to proclaim, or at least predict, a replay of the "Great Game" in the Caucasus and Central Asia. The implication of course is that the driving dynamic of the region, fuelled and lubricated by oil, will be the competition of the great powers. Our goal is to avoid, and actively to discourage, that atavistic outcome'. But Talbot also knew the Game was already on and issued a grim warning to its players, even as he declared that Washington's top priority was conflict resolution. 'If internal and cross-border conflicts simmer and flare, the region could become a breeding ground of terrorism, a hotbed of religious and political extremism and a battleground for outright war'.[8]

The Clinton administration not only openly supported and canvassed for UNOCAL, it appeared in fact that US policy in Afghanistan was intertwined with the fortunes of that company. During two trips to Pakistan and Afghanistan in April and August 1995, the US Assistant Secretary of State for South Asia Robin Raphel spoke in favour of the UNOCAL project. 'We have an American company that is interested in building a pipeline from Turkme nistan to Pakistan', said Raphel at a press conference in

Islamabad in April 1996. 'The pipeline project will be very good for Turkmenistan, for Pakistan and for Afghanistan as it will not only offer job opportunities but also energy in Afghanistan', she added. In August, Raphel visited the Central Asian capitals and Moscow where she pitched the same message. Open support for the UNOCAL project aroused an already suspicious Russia and Iran, which became even more convinced that the CIA was backing the Taliban.[9] When the Taliban captured Kabul in September 1996, Chris Taggert, a UNOCAL executive, told wire agencies that the pipeline project would be easier to implement now that the Taliban had captured Kabul – a statement that UNOCAL quickly retracted because it implied that UNOCAL favoured a Taliban conquest. As mentioned earlier, within hours of Kabul's capture by the Taliban, the US State Department announced it would establish diplomatic relations with the Taliban by sending an official to Kabul – an announcement it retracted just as rapidly. Rashid writes, 'UNOCAL's position was closely linked to US policy on Afghanistan – that it would not construct the pipeline or discuss commercial terms with the Taliban, until there was a recognized government in Afghanistan. UNOCAL's real influence with the Taliban was that their project carried the possibility of US recognition which the Taliban were desperately anxious to secure'. This was made clear in the testimony by John J. Maresca, Vice-President for International Relations of UNOCAL Corporation, before the House Committee on International Relations Sub-Committee on Asia Pacific in which he underlined the significance and intertwining of US commercial interests and US foreign policy in the region. But this was only the public posture.

Basically the USA and UNOCAL accepted the analysis and aims of Pakistan's ISI – that a Taliban victory in Afghanistan would make UNOCAL's job much easier and quicken US recognition. There was criticism from many quarters about linking Afghanistan's future to western oil interests. Among them was the UN. Yasushi Akashi, the UN Under-Secretary General for Humanitarian Affairs told Ahmed Rashid: 'The outside interference in Afghanistan is now all related to the battle for oil and gas pipeline. The fear is that these companies and regional powers are renting the Taliban for their own purposes'.[10]

As mentioned earlier, between 1994 and 1996, the US supported the Taliban politically through its allies Pakistan and Saudi Arabia, essentially because Washington viewed the Taliban as anti-Iranian, anti-Shia and pro-West. The US conveniently ignored the Taliban's own Islamic fundamentalist agenda, its suppression of women and the consternation they created in Central Asia, largely because Washington was not interested in the larger picture. Between 1995 and 1997, US support was even more direct because of its backing for the UNOCAL project. Although there was no CIA budget for providing arms and ammunition to the Taliban and UNOCAL did not channel military support to the Taliban, the US did support the Taliban through its traditional allies Pakistan and Saudi Arabia.

The first public expression of the change in US policy was given by Secretary of State, Madeline Albright, when she visited Islamabad in November 1997. On the steps of Pakistan's Foreign Office she called the Taliban regime 'despicable' for their gender policies. Inside, she warned Pakistani officials that Pakistan was becoming isolated in Central Asia – which weakened US leverage in the region. In 1998 and 1999 the Taliban's support for bin Laden, their refusal to endorse the UNOCAL project or compromise with their opponents and the new moderate government in Iran provided reasons for the US to get tough with the Taliban. By the end of 1998 'getting bin Laden' had become Washington's primary policy objective and it wanted to get him by military means as Taliban refused to co-operate.

Two French analysts have claimed that under the influence of a US oil company, the government of George W. Bush initially blocked intelligence agencies' investigation on terrorism while it bargained with Taliban on the delivery of Osama bin Laden in exchange for political recognition and economic aid.[11] In the book *Bin Laden, La Verite Interdite* (Bin Laden, the Forbidden Truth) the authors Jean Charles Brisard and Guillaume Dasquie reveal that FBI's deputy director John O'Neill resigned in July 2001 to protest over the obstruction. The authors claim that O'Neill told them that 'the main obstacles to investigate Islamic terrorism were US oil corporate interests and the role played by Saudi Arabia in it'. The two claim that the US government's main aim was to consolidate the position of the Taliban regime to obtain access to the oil and gas reserves in Central Asia. They affirm that until August 2001 the US government saw the Taliban as a source of stability in Central Asia that would enable the construction of an oil pipeline across Central Asia. Until now, says the book, 'The oil and gas reserves of Central Asia have been controlled by Russia. The Bush government wanted to change all that'. But confronted with Taliban's refusal to accept US conditions, this rationale of energy security changed into a military one. 'At one time during the negotiations, the US representative told the Taliban "either you accept our offer of a carpet of gold or we bring you under a carpet of bombs"', Brisard said in an interview in Paris. According to the book, the Bush administration began to negotiate with the Taliban immediately after coming into power in February 2001. The US and the Taliban diplomatic representatives met several times in Washington, Berlin and Islamabad. The last meeting between US and Taliban representatives took place in August, five weeks before the attacks in New York and Washington, the analysts maintain.

On May 30, 2002, Hamid Karzai, then Chairman of

Afghanistan's interim administration, Pakistan's President General Pervez Musharraf and President Sapamurat Niyazov of Turkmenistan signed a memorandum of understanding laying out plans to build a 900-mile pipeline that would snake across southern Afghanistan, from Turkmenistan's Daulatabad gas fields to the Pakistani port city of Gwader. While the financial arrangements have to be negotiated it is evident that a virtual security guarantee has been given by the USA.

It is pointed out that Zalmay Khalizad, a member of President Bush's National Security Council and the current US envoy to Afghanistan used to work on behalf of UNOCAL which tried to build a pipeline exporting Turkmen gas through Afghanistan. Back then Khalizad advocated engagement of the ruling Taliban regime. He later became one of the architects of the US military campaign in Afghanistan. 'The people who peddle fossil fuels are the most interested and most active in seeking to influence the United States government', notes John Pike, the Director of GlobalSecurity.org. 'But right now I think the US policy is to keep the pipeline out of Iran at any cost'. Julia Nancy, director of Caspian Services for the Petroleum Finance Corporation, an energy consulting group in Washington DC, told CorpWatch: 'The United States is supporting this talk of a pipeline in an effort to isolate Iran and aggravate the situation. And the Russians want to make sure that oil and gas flows north and not south'.[12]

American opposition to the Iranian route is based on a number of factors. Such a route would considerably strengthen Iran's economy and influence. By getting the Caspian and Central Asian oil to the Gulf, Iran would be able to establish close political and economic ties with the region. With oil transiting from Central Asia to Iranian Gulf ports, Iran would strengthen the position in the Gulf essentially in relation to Saudi Arabia and potentially in relation to Iraq. Emerging as a Central Asian republic would also reinforce Iran's position in relation to the Gulf neighbours. The US wants to deny Iran such advantages.

The prestigious Centre for Defence Information points out that it would be wrong to view the American involvement in the Caspian exclusively through the prism of oil and gas. Military assistance and joint training serve a number of other useful purposes. Prevention of future conflicts in the Caucasus is a goal in its own right regardless of the region's mineral reserves. It does admit, however, that

> Oil reserves in US territory are increasingly scarce while consumption is expected to grow by as much as 25 per cent over the next 20 years, necessitating the search for additional foreign sources of oil. It is the policy of the US to diversify world sources of oil. The idea – reduced dependency on any particular region – thus decreases the possibility that a political upheaval in one country/region will significantly affect oil supplies and bring about a global economic crisis.[13]

Currently many Western governments and the World Bank are only watching the situation and will go in for pipelines only after the internal situation in Afghanistan is stable.

'Escaping the template of Cold War rivalry is proving difficult, even though US-Russian economic interests coincide. Many in the US see Russia through old prisms, despite Moscow's demonstrated commitment to helping the US wage war in Afghanistan and elsewhere', says Anatol Lieven, a regional analyst at the Carnegie Endowment for International Peace in Washington. That some in Washington want to keep US troops in Central America beyond the Afghanistan campaign 'accentuates the fact that the war on terrorism is horribly complicated, and risks being lost by being overloaded with other agendas', Lieven adds.[14]

Moscow's former domains stretch from Uzbekistan to Ukraine, and have often bristled under Russia's strong-arm tactics to re-exert control. The US military presence may be forcing changes. 'The fact that Russia has acquiesced to US troops in Central Asia and indeed Georgia, shows that Russia itself is prepared to play a much more open and even-handed role in the region', says Julian Lee, a senior analyst at the Centre for Global Energy Studies in London. 'But we are seeing Russian interest in business channels, rather than political and military ones. It's the sensible way forward'.[15] The US National Security Adviser Condaleeza Rice had this issue in mind when in an October 15, 2001 interview with the liberal Moscow newspaper *Izvestia*, she went to great lengths to reassure Russian readers that the US has no design on Russia's traditional hegemony over Central Asian oil reserves.

The war in Central Asia, then, has long been in the pipeline, pun intended. As early as 1993, Secretary of State Warren Christopher announced that the Clinton White House would 'advance America's economic security with the same energy and resourcefulness we devoted to waging the Cold War'. War games in 1997 and 1998 coupled with the 1999 Clinton/NATO air war over the former Yugoslavia for Balkan energy pipelines exposed US strategy for the period ahead. Bush's expanding war in Central Asia, establishing military bases in parts of the former Soviet Union, and now his war on Iraq, all this is a logical extension of the Clinton doctrine. America's 'tactical goal' is a conventional military cordon around Central Asia along the borders of the new American empire.

Notes

1. Scott Peterson, *Christian Science Monitor*, March 15, 2002.
2. Eric Mongois, 'War on Terror Masks Bush's Grand Strategy', *Toronto Sun*, March 10, 2002.

3 *BBC Monitoring*, Central Asia Unit, December 10, 2001.

4 *Asia Times*, October 6, 2001.

5 Ahmed Rashid, *Taliban: The Story of the Afghan Warlords*, Pan Books 2001.

6 Ariel Cohne, 'Building a New "Silk Road" to Economic Prosperity: US Policy in the Caucuses and Central Asia', *Heritage Foundation Backgrounder*, July 1997.

7 Michael Klare, *Resource Wars: The New Landscape of Global Conflict*, Metropolitan Books, New York, 2001.

8 Strobe Talbott, 'Deepening US Engagement with the states of Central Asia and the Caucuses', speech in Washington, July 21, 1997.

9 Ahmed Rashid, *Taliban*.

10 Ibid.

11 Julio Goday, *Asia Times*, November 19, 2002.

12 Pratap Chatterji, CorpWatch Inc. June 29, 2002.

13 Centre for Defence Information, 'Terror and Oil in Central Asia', June 13, 2002.

14 Quoted by Scott Peterson, *Christian Science Monitor*, March 15, 2002.

15 *Christian Science Monitor*, March 19, 2002.

8

Palestine and Iraq

Two war fronts were inaugurated in West Asia as soon as the War on Terror was launched. One was against the Palestinian nation by the Israeli Prime Minister Sharon anticipating and receiving full cooperation and support from the US. The other was against Iraq, as a new stage in the US military and political campaign to topple Saddam Hussein.

Most discussions on the terrorist attacks in New York and Washington referred to terrorism's 'Middle Eastern origins'. It can be argued though, that the attacks were responses to US policies in West Asia, particularly its support for Israel, the denial of the rights of the Palestinian people, and the sanctions against Iraq which killed thousands every year, especially children. These policies created a climate in which terrorism found willing and easy recruits. There is no evidence, however, that those who attacked the US genuinely wanted the amelioration of the Palestinian or Iraqi people. Even so, it is indisputable that the Palestinian question is central to any analysis of what is happening in West Asia. It is equally clear that the Palestinian question requires a political answer. However, right from the outset, Washington was determined to respond solely by military means. Israeli Prime Minister Sharon did no better, labelling the Palestinian leader Yassir Arafat 'our bin Laden'.

With the September 11 attacks on the US the second

Palestinian intifada, which started in 2000, actually came to an end. On September 20 of that year, Ariel Sharon, then a Likud leader and Member of Parliament, accompanied by a thousand-strong security force, paid a provocative visit, approved by Prime Minister Barak, to the site of the Al Aqsa mosque. The following day Barak sent another large force of heavily armed police and army to the area and when rocks were thrown by some Palestinians, the police responded with lethal force, killing four and wounding hundreds. Thus began the second intifada. The underlying cause was the tremendous anger and frustration among the population of the Occupied Territories, who saw things getting worse, not better, under the Oslo accords, whose hopes had been shattered and whose patience after 33 years of occupation had reached the boiling point. As a leader of the Palestinian Fatah movement, Mohammed Dahlim, pointed out,

> There was a strategic mistake built into 1993 Oslo Agreement: to go for an interim transitional deal, when the two peoples were ready for a comprehensive peace. The interim period allowed the Israelis to carry on as they had before, pressing ahead with settlements and land expropriation behaving like a classic occupation. There were also constant changes on the Israeli side, which led to the cancellation of agreements and understandings.[1]

Israeli Defence Forces responded to Palestinian demonstrations with lethal force even though, as a UN investigation revealed, they 'endured not a single serious casualty'. Some Palestinians then proceeded to arm themselves and the killing escalated on both sides, though the number of victims, as always, was disproportionately large on the Palestinian side.

Arafat clearly realized that the September 11 terrorist

attacks could be used to intensify the repression of the Palestinians. He was among the early leaders to condemn the attacks. Distancing himself from those on Arab streets who expressed joy in the attacks, he initiated a series of steps, including declaration of a cease-fire with injunction to his forces not to fire, even in self-defence. Martin Indyk, Senior Fellow, Foreign Policy Studies called this 'a silver lining' in the very darkest of clouds in his testimony before the House Committee on International Relations.[2]

The need for a solution of the Palestinian problem, in the context of dealing with terrorism, by recognizing the rights of the Palestinian people could no longer be brushed aside even by the US. For the first time the US government began to speak about a Palestinian state, though in deliberately vague terms. And for the first time the UN Security Council passed a resolution calling for a Palestinian state alongside Israel. A US-sponsored resolution said it was 'affirming a vision of a region where two states Israel and Palestine live side by side within secure and recognized boundaries'. The UN Security Council resolution of March 13, 2002 demanded immediate cessation of all acts of violence including terror, provocation, incitement and destruction and urged Israel and Palestine to take steps toward resuming peace talks.

However, a much-anticipated speech by President Bush on the Israeli-Palestinian conflict made on July 24, 2002, represented a major setback for peace. According to President Bush, Palestine's right to exist – even as a truncated mini-state on the West Bank and Gaza strip – was conditional first and foremost on the removal of Palestinian President Yassir Arafat. As Stephen Zunes pointed out,

> This despite the fact that the Israeli Prime Minister Ariel Sharon is more hard line than Arafat on all outstanding issues of the peace process – final borders, Jewish settlements, the status of

> Jerusalem and refugees. In fact Arafat's positions have been more consistent with international law and UN Security Council Resolutions than the policies of any Likud or Labour-led Israeli governments. But Bush still insists that it is the Palestinians not the Israelis who must replace their elected leadership in order for the peace process to move forward.[3]

And what will be the Palestinians' reward for removing Arafat from leadership? 'The United States of America will support the creation of a Palestinian state whose borders and certain aspects of its sovereignty will be provisional until resolved as part of a final settlement in the Middle East'. Bush has introduced a new concept in state formation: interim independence, temporary borders, and partial sovereignty. As Husein Ibish points out, 'Independence and sovereignty are either fully realized or meaningless'.[4] The notions of true independence and a real end to the occupation are so thoroughly undermined by the conditions attached and the full backing given to an Israeli government that openly opposes these goals, as to be utterly meaningless. Having failed, or rather refused, to offer the only thing that can at this point stop the spiral towards disaster – a clear timetable, guaranteed by the international community to end the Israeli occupation and return to negotiations – Bush has made things only worse.

Levi Grinberg, political analyst and senior lecturer at Ben Guirion University, Israel, points out that

> Since 1977 people have been accustomed to American presidents trying to play the role of 'fair mediators' – pressuring Israel to restrain violence and negotiate with its neighbours. Jimmy Carter mediated between Begin and Sadat. President Reagan brought Israel and PLO to a first cease-fire agreement in 1981, and

> stopped Sharon before occupying Beirut in 1982. George Bush sr. coerced Shamir into the Madrid Conference after the Gulf War and Bill Clinton was best man to Rabin and Arafat. Then and all of a sudden comes a president who not only does not mediate but also unilaterally supports Sharon. This is not only confusing to the Israeli 'peace camp' but places the Palestinian leadership in an awkward position not to mention the rest of the Arab world.[5]

In fact, even before his presidential election, George W. Bush and a number of those holding key positions in his administration had prepared a well-defined agenda of the extreme right wing with regard to the Israeli-Palestinian issue. Bush had established contacts with Ariel Sharon and other hardline Israeli leaders before the elections. Therefore, the change in the US policy with Bush coming to power was not surprising, and had less to do with changes in ground realities and more to do with the ideological stance of the new administration.

Grinberg points out how this understanding between Bush and Sharon 'has developed smoothly since 9/11'. Immediately after September 11, Sharon tried to get on the 'War on Terror' bandwagon, declaring that 'Arafat is our bin Laden'. This position was rejected by the American administration, mainly because the US was planning an attack on Afghanistan and did not want to endanger the expected cooperation with the pro-American Arab states. However, during the war in Afghanistan, the Bush administration was disappointed with the position of Saudi Arabia and Egypt. After the 'regime change' in Afghanistan, Sharon was invited to Washington 'to co-ordinate the next moves in the war against terror' – this time against Iraq. In his meeting with President Bush on December 3, 2001, Sharon received a 'green light' to attack Arafat. On December 4, Arafat's helicopters were bombed and he was placed in a 'city arrest' in Ramallah for five months.

Since December 3, President Bush has defined Israel's actions against the Palestinians as 'self-defence' and the Palestinian actions as 'terror'. In going for war against Afghanistan, the US had claimed it was acting in self-defence against the 'terror' from that country. When the UN Security Council decided to send an inquiry committee to investigate war crimes committed in Jenin in April 2002, the US collaborated with the Israeli government in preventing the committee's entry into Israel. On May 7, 2002, on the eve of a meeting with President Bush, in his speech to the Anti-Defamation League in Washington, Sharon claimed, 'There is a moral equivalency and direct connection between America's continuous operations against Al Qaeda in Afghanistan and Operation Defence Shield and any other Israeli Defence operation to defeat terrorists'. He added, 'They are acts of self-defence against the same forces of evil and darkness bent on destroying civilized society'. Israeli military actions against Palestinians thus became part of the US-led War on Terror. And this, in turn, has fed Palestinian resentment:

> Far from setting out a vision of peace, President Bush's plan for Middle East points instead to an American decision to give up on the peace process. What has effectively been done is to transform a series of demands of international community and international law into a series of demands to be made on Yassir Arafat. It also gives a new meaning to democracy where our leaders are to be chosen by others.[6]

Bush complained that 'Today, the elected Palestinian legislature has no authority, and power is concentrated in the hands of an unaccountable few'. He observed, quite correctly, that

'The Palestinian parliament should have the full authority of a legislative body'. 'What he left out', as Ali Abunimah points out 'is that it was the Oslo Accords, signed with the full blessing of the United States that explicitly limited the powers of the Palestinian legislature and gave the Israeli military authorities the right to annul any law passed by it'.[7] On the issue of violence, Bush made it clear that only the Palestinians must renounce it. Israel was given a free hand to 'continue to defend herself'. Palestinians are required to stop 'terror immediately', but Bush only called on Israel to withdraw its forces to the positions held prior to September 28, 2000, and stop settlement construction in the Occupied Territories, 'as we make progress'. This is essentially a license for Israel to carry on with aggressive violence unilaterally, since the settlement building enterprise is based solely on violence – the violent expropriation of Palestinian land, the violent demolition of Palestinian homes – which Sharon has openly declared will continue until he can bring a million more Jews to settle all of 'Judea and Samaria'.

When Bush speaks about Israeli 'occupation', it is merely a word, an abstraction. It is not a system of foreign military dictatorship over millions of people that is the very antithesis of every democratic value Bush claims to stand for and which invades every transaction of daily life. Most incredibly, he views it not as a condition affecting the Palestinians but as something that harms Israelis, because 'permanent occupation threatens Israel's identity and democracy'.

Significantly, President Bush did not mention the peace plan of Saudi Prince Abdullah proposed in February 2002 – endorsed by the Palestinian Authority and every single Arab government – which offered Israel security guarantees and full normal relations in return for withdrawal from the Occupied Territories seized in the 1967 war. The Abdullah plan is largely a reiteration of UN

Security Council Resolutions 242 and 338, long considered by the US as the basis for Middle East peace. Israel has claimed all along that these resolutions do not require it to withdraw from virtually all of the Arab lands conquered 35 years ago. This claim is utterly false and is rejected by almost the entire international community. While the President mentioned the UN resolutions briefly in his speech, he failed to challenge Israel's false claims in this regard.

While many Palestinians are deeply disappointed over Arafat's leadership, President Bush's insistence that the US has the right to determine who shall lead the Palestinians has bred enormous resentment in the Arab world. Israeli Foreign Minister Shimon Peres, upon hearing President Bush's speech was quoted in Israel's largest daily *Yediot Aharonot* as declaring that 'making the creation of a Palestinian state dependent upon a change in the Palestinian leadership is a fatal mistake – the abyss into which the region will plunge will be as deep as the expectations from the speech were high'. Dahlim pointed out that 'Bush is now effectively demanding a *coup d'état* against Arafat because the American administration says that even if he is re-elected it will not deal with him'. And Levi Grinberg pointed out that 'The Bush administration adopted and augmented Sharon's big lie that Arafat is the problem (not the thirty-five-year Israeli occupation) and that a Palestinian state would be established later on (when, where and how remain constantly deferred questions)'. As Grinberg puts it,

> Sharon is deeply satisfied with Bush's Middle East plan that practically means a global war managed by the 'Busharon' team in which Bush will play the role of the global Sheriff, imposing a new order in the Islamic states. Sharon has been nominated as the 'regional Sheriff' and allowed to impose a new order in his area of influence.

Bush's speech was a formal declaration of recognition of Sharon's war against the Palestinians as 'official' part of the war on terror.

It appears quite natural that a US-led global war intended to re-order the world has Iraq as one of its main targets. For a long time in the Washington establishment, there was deep disappointment that in spite of the success of the Gulf War with the declaration of the 'New World Order' by President Bush sr. in 1991 and the continuing crippling sanctions against Iraq, Saddam Hussein remained in power. The administration determined to use the opportunity given by the September 11 events to settle the issue finally. From that fateful day onwards various officials of the administration, including President Bush, directly and indirectly indicated that the US intended to effect a 'regime change' in Iraq. In September 2001 itself, Bush referred to Saddam Hussein as an 'evil man' and said he was 'closely watched'. In fact there is enough evidence that as soon as the new administration assumed office, the hawks in the Pentagon and the State Department began to make plans for a military attack on Iraq.

Several senior officials in the new administration had for long maintained that Saddam Hussein should be removed from power. In January 1998 Donald Rumsfeld (now Defence Secretary) and Paul Wolfowitz (now his deputy) joined by Richard Armitage (now Deputy Secretary of State), John Bolton and Paula Dobriansky (now Under Secretaries of State), Peter Rodman (now Assistant Secretary of Defence), Robert Zoellick (now US Trade Representative) and Richard Perle (now a senior Bush adviser) wrote an open letter to then President Bill Clinton stating:

> We are writing you because we are convinced that current American policy toward Iraq is not succeeding, and that we may soon face a threat in the Middle East more serious than any we have known since the end of the Cold War. We urge you to

> enunciate a new strategy that would secure the interests of the US and our friends and allies around the world. That strategy should aim, above all, at the removal of Saddam Hussein from power.[8]

Soon after the terrorist attacks in New York and Washington vigorous attempts were made by the administration to link Iraq to the terrorists and Al Qaeda. There was, however, no evidence for this whatsoever. The best that CIA Director George Tenet could come up with in a testimony before Congress was that the 'mutual antipathy' that Iraq and Al Qaeda have for the US 'suggests that tactical cooperation between the two is possible'. Most observers considered this to be an extraordinarily weak justification for war against Iraq. The other pretext for the attack on Iraq that Bush used was the danger of Iraq's weapons of mass destruction. Here again there is no proof. The UN inspection teams failed to find anything incriminating against the Iraqi regime both in 1998 as well as 2003. But none of this has prevented conservative defence and security experts from demanding that a strike against Iraq should be an indispensable aspect of the War on Terror. A September 20, 2001, letter to President Bush, published in the neo-conservative *Weekly Standard* and signed by 37 well-known policy experts and columnists made the point in the clearest of terms:

> It may be that the Iraqi government provided assistance in some form to the recent attack on the United States. But even if evidence does not link Iraq directly to the attack, any strategy aiming at the eradication of terrorism and its sponsors must include a determined effort to remove Saddam Hussein from power in Iraq. Failure to undertake such an effort will constitute an early and perhaps decisive surrender in the war on international terrorism.

As early as May 2002, there existed an American military planning document that called for air, land, and sea-based forces to attack Iraq from three directions – the north, south and west – in a campaign to topple President Saddam Hussein:

> The existence of the document that outlined significant aspects of a 'concept' for a war against Iraq . . . indicates an advanced state of planning in the military. The concept for such a plan is now highly evolved and is apparently working its way through the military channels. Once a consensus is reached on the concept, the steps toward assembling a final war plan and, most importantly, the element of timing for ground deployments and commencement of an air war, represent the final sequencing that Mr Bush will have to decide.[9]

It was around the same time as the 'war plan' document was leaked that the third round of talks between the United Nations and Iraq on weapons inspection was held in Vienna. Iraq blamed the US for breakdown in the talks accusing it of looking to escalate the issue as part of its plan to topple the regime of Saddam Hussein. Iraq charged that Washington was insisting on a return of arms inspectors only to assist its planned military action against Iraq. Iraq linked the return of inspectors to the lifting of sanctions and to an end to US military threats. Indeed, the Gulf War cease-fire resolution of the Security Council specified that sanctions will be lifted when the disarmament mandate is completed. From the outset, however, Washington made it clear that even total co-operation with the United Nations Special Commission (UNSCOM) would not lead to an end to the sanctions. Both Clinton and Bush and their senior officials have made it clear that the US would agree to lift sanctions only after Saddam Hussein is ousted from power. The promise to lift sanctions in return for compliance with weapons inspections would have been a powerful inducement for Iraqi cooperation. It could have helped to resolve the dispute over weapons and end the prolonged sanctions-related suffering of the Iraqi people. As David Cortright pointed out in August 2002,

> The debate about weapons inspections will be crucial to the prospects for war. The United States might attempt to take advantage of the inspections issue to build support for military action. If Baghdad refuses to permit inspections or if it places new obstacles in their way, Washington might provoke a crisis by issuing an ultimatum. Iraq's refusal to comply with such an ultimatum could then become the pretext for war.[10]

Scott Ritter, who led the UNSCOM team in Iraq for seven years, said: 'claims that Iraq is rearming came from unreliable witnesses' adding that 'factories bombed in 1998 Operation Desert Fox had not breached UN resolutions. . . . Every one of these facilities was subjected to repeated inspection and never did we detect anything remotely to suggest that these were involved in producing anything prohibited. There's nothing there. Nothing'.[11]

After weeks of negotiations the UN Security Council unanimously adopted in November 2002, a tough resolution on Iraq giving it a 'final opportunity to comply with its disarmament obligations' or face 'serious consequences'. While the US made some major concessions to critics during the long-drawn out negotiations on the resolution, the final resolution still met the Bush administration's key demands: toughening UN weapons inspection and leaving the US free to take military action against Iraq if inspectors say Baghdad is not complying. The inspectors were to have 'unconditional and unrestricted access' to all sites including eight presidential compounds.

Resolution 1441 said that Iraq 'has been and remains in material breach of earlier UN resolutions'. The resolution appeared to be a triumph for the UN, but it was a triumph fraught with ambiguities. Its unanimous passage, including the assent of France, Russia and even Syria, did not signal international consensus so much as willingness to interpret the document differently and resolve the differences if at some later date Iraq violated the agreement.

Top officials of the Bush administration repeatedly stated, after the resolution was passed, that the US did not need the 'permission' of the United Nations to go after Iraq in any military fashion. 'The UN can meet and discuss, but we don't need their permission', the Joint Chief of Staff Andrew Card stated on November 10, 2002. Secretary of State Colin Powell also spoke along the same lines in an interview to the CNN: 'If we find that the debate is not going anywhere, if the UN chooses not to act, we have not given up our authority to act with like-minded nations who might wish to join us in such a mission'.

However taking into account the unprecedented worldwide protests and the serious opposition the British Prime Minister was facing at home, the US, UK and Spain introduced a resolution in the Security Council on February 24, 2003. The resolution recalled that the Security Council's 'resolution 1441, while acknowledging that Iraq has been and remains in material breach of its obligations, afforded Iraq a final opportunity to comply with its disarmament obligations under relevant resolutions' and 'Decides that Iraq has failed to take the final opportunity afforded to it in resolution 1441'. An alternate proposal was made by France, Russia and Germany on the same day. This Memorandum said, 'The Security Council must step up its efforts to give a real chance to the peaceful settlement of the crisis', and concluded, 'The combination of a clear programme of action, reinforced inspections, a clear timeline and the military build-up provide a realistic means to reunite the Security Council and to exert maximum pressure on Iraq'.

For months the attention of much of the world focused on the diplomatic exercises in the Security Council and the scope and results of the inspection process. This led many observers to conclude that the pace and timing of the war against Iraq will be largely determined by the dynamics of diplomatic debate in the UN. However, as others had feared, it is not diplomacy but the military and logistical factors in the Pentagon preparations that determined the timing of the attack on Iraq. The political decision to attack Iraq was made months before the Security Council debate and the military build-up had been going on since that time.

No convincing case has been made for a war against Iraq. All attempts by the US to show any links between Iraq and Al Qaeda failed. The imperial arrogance of the US has divided NATO, split the European Union and caused serious disagreements within the UN Security Council. It did not eventually turn out that way, but even so it is perhaps useful to remind ourselves that a UN-backed war on Iraq under the same circumstances would have been as immoral and unjust as the one plotted in the Pentagon because it would still have been the same war. The questionable moral character of a preemptive strike, an intervention and a unilateral action is compounded by a policy that involves all three. Moreover the fact that great powers set precedent in world politics means that each choice they make must be measured by the consequences of the precedent they set.

On February 26, 2003, President Bush in a speech at the American Enterprise Institute, Washington DC, spoke of the 'rebuilding' of Iraq after the war comparing it to US efforts after the Second World War to rebuild war-ravaged countries including wartime enemies Germany and Japan. Creating a 'free and peaceful

Iraq' will be a difficult task requiring a 'sustained commitment' from the US and other countries but a new Iraq could serve 'a dramatic and inspiring example of freedom' throughout the Middle East, President Bush said. The speech reinforced the view that the US already had a blueprint for a post-Saddam Iraq after 'occupation and regime change'. The question that remains is how long Iraq would be under direct US military control. Marvan Bishara warns:

> The Bush administration should be careful when it talks about democracy in the Middle East. The idea is too valuable and too vital to be used as cynical camouflage for other agendas whether these are based on oil interests or Israel or the desire to have a solid military beachhead in a volatile region. War would lead to regime change in Iraq but rather than bring democracy it would probably lead to chaos, the enemy of democracy in a land that continues to suffer from tribal, ethnic and religious divisions.[12]

In his speech to the American Enterprise Institute, Bush also mentioned the other war front in West Asia. He said, 'Success in Iraq could also begin a new stage for Middle Eastern peace and set in motion progress towards a truly democratic Palestinian state. As for Israel [its] new government – as the terror threat is removed and security improves – will be expected to support the creation of a viable state and to work as quickly as possible toward a final status agreement', surprisingly omitting mention of the three-year timeline which he had set for Palestinian independence in June 2002.

Bush also reiterated his support for the 'road map' that is being worked out by the so-called Quartet – the US, the UN, the EU and Russia – to expedite Palestinian independence and ensure Israeli security. The US administration has resisted pressure from other members of the Quartet to make the 'road map' – which Sharon has rejected as meaningless – public as a way of offering hope to the Palestinian population that a viable independent state is within their grasp. *The New York Times* wrote editorially the next day, February 27, that 'Bush's rhetorical support for the initiative appears to amount to little more than lip service'. The President put Iraq in the centre of the picture arguing that 'success there would deprive Palestinian terrorists of critical support and provide Palestinian people with an inspiration for establishing their own democratic institutions'. To President Bush the Palestinian issue is one of terrorism supported by Iraq and its resolution will be when 'the terror threat is removed'. This is exactly the position of Ariel Sharon.

In March 2003, the US, UK and Spain, faced with the prospect of their resolution being vetoed in the Security Council, withdrew the resolution. President Bush issued an ultimatum to Saddam Hussein and his sons to leave Iraq. When he refused to do so, the US, in the face of overwhelming world opinion, launched the attack on Iraq. There are many reasons for the widespread opposition to military action in Iraq. The first and foremost is the lack of any justification for war. Iraq has not attacked or credibly threatened the US. Its weapons programme, while a serious concern, does not pose an immediate threat to neighbouring countries or the US. Under international law one country is justified in attacking another country only when it is under attack or about to be under attack. There is no *casus belli* here. Second, the potential human cost of the war. It is estimated that tens of thousands of Iraqis could die in such a conflict, and casualties among US forces might be significant. Third, the war in Iraq, which is being fought as these lines are being drafted, could lead to the very use of weapons of mass destruction that the Bush administration says it wants to prevent. US claims about Iraqi weapons are greatly exaggerated, but it is not unlikely that Baghdad retains some chemical and biological weapons capability. If pushed to the wall Saddam Hussein might just decide to use them. The Pentagon's new doctrine, as articulated in the 'Nuclear Posture Review', envisions the use of nuclear weapons by the US for precisely such contingencies – to counter the development or use of weapons of mass destruction by states like Iraq in the 'Axis of Evil'. Fourth, the political damage that would result from the war. The US and UK, in spite of their brave talk of an 'ever growing coalition of the willing' are acting pretty much alone, and in the face of strong opposition from many nations, especially in the Arab world. The political rage sparked by an American war could destabilize governments in the region and will certainly increase turmoil and political extremism throughout the Middle East and beyond. And fifth, the US military campaign against Iraq has set a dangerous precedent of pre-emptive attack that violates the Charter of the United Nations and undermines the very foundations of international law.

During the Gulf War, the US was able to repel a great deal of the criticism that it would have otherwise received, because it had the support of major segments of the international community, including most of the Arab states. Unlike in 1991, when most of the region supported – and even contributed to – the US-led war, Arab opposition is strong today and Washington's attack on Iraq seen as unjustified. The Arab League has voiced its strong opposition to the war and in many Arab countries vast sections of the population have demonstrated against the war. There is also growing criticism in the Arab world about the facilities offered by Kuwait, Qatar and Bahrain to the US-led coalition forces. Half of Kuwait has been converted to a military base for these forces and it is from here that the ground battle against Iraq is launched.

It should be recalled in this connection that Kuwait had actually reconciled with Iraq an year ago. In March 2002, Iraq and Kuwait signed a document written by Kuwaiti Foreign Minister Sheik Sabah Al Ahmed in which Iraq for the first time formally consented to respect the sovereignty of Kuwait. Sabah declared that his country was 100 per cent satisfied with the agreement, and Kuwait reiterated its opposition to US plans for invasion of Iraq. Saudi Arabia's Crown Prince Abdullah called the pact a 'very positive achievement' and expressed confidence that Iraq would uphold the agreement. However, rather than welcoming this breakthrough, State Department spokesman Richard Boucher declared that the US was 'profoundly sceptical' of the accord. By becoming the operational base for an illegal war, Kuwait is violating international laws.

The US insistence on the right to attack Iraq unilaterally has effectively undermined the principle of collective security and the authority of the United Nations and could encourage international anarchy. If Iraq's neighbours or the US had felt threatened by Iraq, any of these countries could have approached the Security Council and made their case as to how and why their security was threatened. Iraq's neighbours have not done so subsequent to 1991, apparently, because they have not felt threatened.

As this book goes to press, the war in Iraq is winding down and the Saddam Hussein regime is gone. However, it is clear, given the Afghanistan experience, that throwing out a government is easier than putting a new one together. European diplomats agree that 'the integrity of Iraq is the most important consideration of all. It's vital for Turkey, Iran, Syria, Saudi Arabia all the important regional players'. The common nightmare is a post-Saddam Hussein fragmentation.[13] As the European Union's external affairs chief

Chris Patten warned: 'The Afghan war has reinforced some dangerous instincts: that the projection of military power is the only basis of true security, that the US can rely on no one but itself, and that allies may be useful as optional extras'. America's Arab allies have expressed concern that an Iraq without a strong central government could disintegrate into Shia Arab, Sunni Arab, and Kurdish mini-states. And there is no doubt that a long drawn out occupation of Iraq by American forces will lead to very widespread resentment and anger all over the region.

As in Central Asia, the reordering by the War on Terror has other objectives in the Iraq campaign also. The removal of President Saddam Hussein would open Iraq's rich new oilfields to western bidders and bring the prospect of lessening dependence on Saudi oil. No other country offers such untapped oilfields whose exploitation could lessen tensions over the western presence in Saudi Arabia. President Bush has used the War on Terror to press his case for drilling in protected Arctic refuge, but predicted reserves in Alaska are dwarfed by the oil wells of the Gulf. Anthony Cordesman, of the Centre for Strategic and International Studies in Washington said the issue for the US was as much the security of the Gulf as access to particular oilfields. As Michael T. Klare observed, 'As I see it, then, the removal of Saddam Hussein and his replacement by someone beholden to the United States is a key part of a broader strategy aimed at assuring permanent American global dominance'.[14] Or as Michael Igantieff put it in his seminal essay on America's emerging empire, the concentration of so much oil in the Gulf 'makes it what a military strategist would call the "empire's centre of gravity"'.[15] Gerald Butt, Gulf editor of the *Middle East Economic Review*, said: 'The removal of Saddam is, in effect, the removal of the last threat to the free flow of oil from the Gulf as a whole'. Three giant southern fields – Majnoon, West Qurna and Nahr Umar have the capacity to produce as much as Kuwait. The first two could each equal Qatar's production of 700,000 barrels a day. 'There is nothing like it anywhere else in the world. It's the big prize'.[16]

Notes

1 Mohammed Dahlim, *Guardian*, July 2, 2002.
2 Martin Indyk, testimony before Sub-Committee on Middle East and South Asia, September 25, 2001.
3 Stephen Zunes, 'Bush's Speech a Setback for Peace', *Foreign Policy in Focus*, June 26, 2002.
4 Hussein Ibish in the *Los Angeles Times*, June 20, 2002.
5 Levi Grinberg, 'The Busharon Global War', *Foreign Policy in Focus*, June 2002.
6 Mohammed Dahlim, *Guardian*, July 2, 2002.
7 Ali Abinumah, 'Bush's Speech a Vision of Permanent War', *Electronic Intifada,* June 25, 2002.
8 *Asia Times*, October 13, 2002.
9 Eric Schmitt, *New York Times*, July 5, 2002. This document outlines the concept 'as it stood about two months ago'.
10 David Cortright, 'Stop the War Before it Starts', *The Progressive*, August 2002.
11 Interview to the Scottish daily *The Herald*, July 8, 2002.
12 Marvan Bishara in the *International Herald Tribune*, February 27, 2003.
13 *Asia Times*, July 9, 2002.
14 *Foreign Policy in Focus*, January 16, 2003.
15 'The Burden', *The New York Times Magazine*, January 5, 2003.
16 Michael Thodoulu and Ronald Watson, 'West Sees Glittering Prizes in Giant Oil Fields', *The Times of London*, July 11, 2002.

9

The 'Allies' in South Asia

In the vaguely defined international coalition in the War on Terror, India and Pakistan occupy acutely uncomfortable positions. Pakistan was an ally of the US during the Cold War, and India, an important leader of the Non-Aligned Movement, was seen as an obstacle to US goals and objectives in the region. Throughout the 1990s, American relations with India warmed, while relations with Pakistan cooled. Prior to September 11, Pakistan was one of three countries to recognize the Taliban regime in Afghanistan, which came to power with its active support. India, on the other hand, had ties to the anti-Taliban Northern Alliance. By warming up to Pakistan in the aftermath of the attacks, the US reversed the tilt toward India for which it had assiduously worked for some three years, apparently favouring its 'tactical ally' Pakistan over its 'natural ally' India.

Ironically the two countries, which found themselves on the same side in the US-led War on Terror, entered a new phase of mutual rivalry leading to heightened tension. In the context of the War on Terror, the hostility between India and Pakistan was going to be played out on different planes: Kashmir, nuclear weapons, and Afghanistan itself.

India was one of the first countries to declare unequivocal support to the US War on Terror. Immediately after the September 11 attacks, India's Foreign Minister Jaswant Singh offered unsolicited, unlimited military co-operation, including the use of airbases, to the US. Despite opposition even from some of his cabinet colleagues, Home Minister Advani reiterated the government's offer of bases and logistical support to the US. Washington, however, appeared to be indifferent to the offer. General Pervez Musharraf, too, offered to be America's staunch ally if India and Israel were kept out of the alliance. For obvious geo-strategic reasons for the first stage of the War on Terror, it was Pakistan's facilities that the US needed most. The statements by the heads of governments of India and Pakistan on the War on Terror formalized the beginning of a new stage of hostility between two allies of the US.

Indian Prime Minister Atal Behari Vajpayee's October 2, 2001 letter to President Bush was an eloquent mix of obsequiousness towards the US and hawkishness towards Pakistan. Accusing Pakistan of harbouring terrorists, the Prime Minister said, 'Pakistan must understand that there is a limit to the patience of the people of India', a statement he repeated several times in the coming months. The Indian Foreign Minister and Home Minister enthusiastically applauded President Bush's 'with us or with the terrorists' speech, his first declaration of war. At work in New Delhi was the calculated dismantling of the entire rationale of non-alignment and the edifice of an independent foreign policy, and subjugation of India's national interests to US war plans.

As the US prepared for retribution against the perpetrators of the September 11 attacks, Pakistan was among the first nations it turned its attention to. Literally at gunpoint, the military establishment was asked to stand up and be counted as a supporter of the new war on terrorism or be treated on a par with the terrorists. Recognizing that Islamabad's cooperation would be vital for any operation in Afghanistan, the Bush administration offered Pakistan both carrots and sticks. Washington made numerous demands of Islamabad, including military and intelligence cooperation, termination of the flow of volunteers and fuel supplies to Afghanistan and end of support to the Taliban. The US conveyed in unambiguous terms that any reservations on the part of Islamabad would be deemed as a hostile act and the consequences would be unimaginable. Left with no choice, the military ruler and self-appointed President, General Pervez Musharraf, immediately agreed to be coopted, despite all the pulls and pressures from within his country.

In return for Pakistan's cooperation, Washington quickly lifted nuclear sanctions, suspended the 'democracy' sanctions imposed after the 1999 coup and put together a package of nearly $1 billion in debt relief. Nuclear sanctions on India too were lifted, but India did not like the idea of being treated on a par with Pakistan. India had expected its sanctions alone would be lifted.

In a clever and brilliantly delivered speech, the Pakistani President virtually told the people of Pakistan that he had chosen to side with the US as the very integrity of the nation was at stake. While Musharraf made the choice within hours of the call from Washington, it took him eight days to take the nation into confidence on the factors he claimed had compelled him to side with the international community (read the US) in its efforts to combat terrorism. He accused India of hatching a conspiracy to curry favour with the US and get Pakistan declared a terrorist state:

> Let us now take a look at the designs of our neighbouring country. They offered all their military facilities to the US. They have offered, without hesitation, all their facilities, all their bases and full logistic support. They want to enter into an alliance with the US and get Pakistan declared a terrorist state. They want to harm our strategic assets and the Kashmir cause.[1]

The General listed what he termed as four specific critical concerns and priorities that guided his government's decision to become once again the forward-line state for the superpower. These were security of the country and external threat; the economy and its revival, strategic nuclear and missile assets, and the Kashmir cause.

It was clear that Musharraf was unaware of US war aims in Afghanistan at that stage. He asked the Taliban to change their policy. Musharraf believed he had the right to ask them because of the relentless campaign by Islamabad in support of the Taliban when the entire world was against them. He had advice for the Americans too:

> We are telling the Americans too that they should be patient. Whatever their plans, they should be cautious and balanced. We are asking them to come up with whatever evidence they have against Osama bin Laden. What I would like to know is how we could save Afghanistan and the Taliban. And how do we ensure that they suffer minimum losses.

At that time Musharraf did not know that the US wanted to oust the Taliban from power. A little later he thought that at least the 'moderate' elements in the Taliban could find a place in the new Afghan dispensation. He was wrong on that too.

For Pakistan the time of reckoning had come a day sooner than later. The myth of 'strategic depth', the pet phrase of the military establishment about Afghanistan, had been exploded. Afghanistan had been a crucial component of Pakistan's foreign policy for nearly three decades. It was unravelling. Pakistan had used Taliban as a support base for its Kashmir policy. That had adversely affected Pakistan's social base.

India and Pakistan entered into an intense competition to benefit from the shifts in American policy, which followed the

September 11 attack. The Indian government had sought a closer engagement with the US and in spite of the sanctions imposed after the nuclear tests of May 1998, had benefited from an American tilt toward New Delhi underlined by President Clinton's visit to India in March 2000. This American connection was important to the Bharatiya Janata Party (BJP), which leads the Indian ruling coalition, for practical and ideological reasons. It put Pakistan at a disadvantage. It fitted with the BJP's neo-liberal economic policies, and it played to the BJP's vision – or illusion – of India as a great power that could speak to the US on equal terms.

September 11 brought immediate attention to Pakistan, restoring an old US relationship, and turning the aid and trade tap back on for the Musharraf regime. Pakistan's disadvantage was ended. America needed Pakistan in its war on Afghanistan. This caused considerable annoyance to India. But the War on Terror also deepened India's relationship with the US. South Asia had become what the BJP had always wished it to be – an area of great strategic importance to the region – and India was by far the biggest and strongest state in the region. But the US, India and Pakistan though all part of the War on Terror had different views on terrorism and different purposes for the war.

India has been the regional 'sore winner' as Stephen P. Cohen says:

> Although it took no joy in seeing America restore its relationship with Pakistan after the September 11 attacks, the renewed link ultimately turned to New Delhi's advantage. The US lifted the [nuclear-related] sanctions on India too. The United States also exerted heavy pressure on Islamabad to cease its support for cross-border movement from Pakistan to Kashmir and pressed Islamabad to crack down on Islamic radicals – many of whom were targeting India. Washington accelerated the pace of

> rapprochement between the two once-estranged democracies. Indian American military cooperation increased dramatically, earlier plans for defence cooperation were revived and big US military sales to India were soon in the offing.[2]

After a terrorist attack on India's parliament building on December 13, 2001, and India's accusation of Pakistan's complicity in it through the Pakistan-based Lashkar-i-Taiba (Army of the Pure), tensions mounted and brought the two countries to the brink of war. Indian leaders of the ruling National Democratic Alliance (NDA) indulged in a high-decibel campaign demanding that Pakistan hand over to India 20 'wanted terrorists'. Unsurprisingly, Pakistan refused to do so, which led India to deploy in very large numbers troops at the border. This brought the subcontinent on the brink of war.

However, there was considerable easing of tensions by the beginning of 2002. In his message to the nation, the Indian Prime Minister Vajpayee reiterated the vision of peace in the subcontinent that marked his message of the previous New Year. 'In our search for a lasting solution to the Kashmir problem, both in its external and internal dimensions, we shall not traverse solely on the beaten track of the past. Rather, we shall be bold and innovative designers of a future architecture of peace and prosperity for the entire South Asian region'.[3]

The Indian Prime Minister's statesmanship proved to be unfortunately short-lived. Under obvious pressure from sections of his own party, he soon did a volte face and not only talked of war, but also of using of any weapons, obviously including nuclear weapons. *The Hindu* wrote editorially:

> Mr Vajpayee in a manner befitting more a rabble-rousing politician, has spoken in terms that are associated with a state

of war. Almost in the same breath as making a reference to India going ahead with the nuclear tests in the face of stiff international opposition and sanctions, the Prime Minister declared that 'no weapon' would be spared in self-defence. And for good measure, he also reportedly said that it was time that India gave a 'reply' to Pakistan. Such hawkish rhetoric, apart from undermining as it does the basic objective of sensitizing the peoples of both India and Pakistan to the menace of terrorism, does not exactly square with the sort of statesmanship required at the present critical juncture, both on the Indo-Pakistan and international fronts.[4]

An important address to the nation by the Pakistani leader Musharraf on January 14 appeared to mark a historic turning point for Pakistan. He confronted the challenges before Pakistan, both foreign and domestic, in an ambitious and forward-looking style. He announced new measures to crack down on Islamic militants who have fomented terrorism in Pakistan and abroad. He set forth a vision of Pakistan as an example of a tolerant and progressive form of Islam. General Musharraf struck a balance in his speech, particularly in his remarks addressed to India, between conciliation and brusque warnings of Pakistan's readiness to defend itself. Devoting barley two minutes of his hour-long speech to the Kashmir issue, he wrapped his pledge of an end to terrorism in blunt words for India's leaders.

In the remarks he addressed to the US, he said it was America's responsibility to put pressure on India to negotiate a settlement of the Kashmir dispute. The pact between the US and Pakistan had put the former in a fix about Kashmir. India equated Pakistan's support for Islamic militant groups fighting in Kashmir with its backing for the Taliban and insisted that General Musharraf could not make war on terrorism on Pakistan's western frontier in

Afghanistan, and support it on its eastern border, in Kashmir.

The War on Terror has taught the world a number of lessons. Among the most important is that long-term conflicts cannot be allowed to fester indefinitely. The conflict between India and Pakistan over Kashmir is among the most intractable in the world. Ethnicity, religion, nationalism, state repression, systematic human rights violations and terrorism are important ingredients of this complex issue.

Two factors brought a greater focus to the Kashmir issue in the context of the War on Terror. The first is geography. The war in Afghanistan has made South Asia the world's new fault line in the War against Terror. Yet, terror is in the eye of the beholder. India, which controls much of Kashmir, sees the conflict as a battle against terrorism. Pakistan views it as a war of liberation. The vast military implications are another crucial factor. Both India and Pakistan are fledgling nuclear powers.

Following a major terrorist attack inside Kashmir the two countries again came to the brink of war in June 2002 raising the possibility of a nuclear war, which would have disastrous consequences. The India-Pakistan military stand-off of 2002 is undoubtedly one of the gravest among many that have marked the continuing hostility between the two nations. The armed forces of the two countries faced each other across the border eyeball to eyeball from January 2002. But what has disturbingly distinguished this from all previous ones is the recurring reference to the possible use of nuclear weapons heard from both sides.

The threat of nuclear weapons has been brandished by the highest levels of political leadership from both sides with occasional denials or modifications. As already mentioned, in the midst of India's preparations for war following the attack on the parliament in December 2001, the Indian Prime Minister made a clear reference to the possible use of nuclear weapons. Speaking to a gathering of the party faithful, the Prime Minister declared: 'No weapon would be spared in self-defence. Whatever weapon was available it would be used no matter how it wounded the enemy'.[5] Defence Minister George Fernandes, even while claiming that nuclear deterrence would hold between India and Pakistan, and that Pakistan's leadership would not risk nuclear confrontation, expressed himself in remarkably hawkish terms: 'We could take strike, survive, and then hit back. Pakistan would be finished'.[6] More recently, the provocation from the Indian side has come mostly in the form of repeated calls for a 'decisive battle' to deal with the problem 'once and for all'. Although these statements have been made with reference to Pakistan's sponsorship and support for cross-border terrorism, the tone has an unmistakably nuclear pitch.

Pakistan has always maintained that nuclear weapons are its ultimate guarantee for territorial integrity against the conventional superiority of India. General Musharraf stated in an interview to the German magazine *Der Speigel* that nuclear weapons are part of the calculation, especially if Pakistan is threatened with extinction. The statements by the leaders of the two countries provoked widespread international criticism and as a result both stepped back from the rhetoric about nuclear weapons. On May 30, 2002, Musharraf offered the guarantee that his country will not initiate a nuclear war. On June 1, in an interview to the CNN, he insisted that Pakistan had made no forward deployment of nuclear missile and expressed his confidence that neither side would be irresponsible enough to initiate nuclear confrontation. From the Indian side also there were statements dismissing the possibility of a nuclear war.

The fact, though, is that the nuclear arms race in the subcontinent was initiated by India after its nuclear test in May 1998. The Indian nuclear weapons programme was clearly Pakistan-centric. Pakistan quickly followed suit. Indian leaders made early on an explicit and provocative linkage between nuclear weaponization and the most contentious issue in India-Pakistan relations, Kashmir. Home Minister Advani said on May 18, 1998: 'India's decisive step to become a nuclear weapon state has brought about a qualitatively new stage in Indo-Pak relations, particularly in finding a lasting solution to the Kashmir problem', and called upon the Pakistan government to 'realize the change in the geo-strategic situation in the region and the world'.[7] Musharraf's address to the nation in the wake of the September 11 attacks clearly showed that in Pakistan too, nuclear weapons were linked to the Kashmir issue. Referring to India he said, as already mentioned, 'They also want our strategic assets and our Kashmir cause to be harmed'. Strategic assets, in this instace, are nuclear weapons.

The nuclear games of the subcontinental neighbours call into question America's own nuclear stance. The fact that the US has withdrawn from the Anti-Ballistic Missile Treaty, is pursuing new and more useable 'mini' nuclear weapons, changing the deterrence doctrine and is committed to deploying a multi-tiered ballistic missile defence are not lost on Indian and Pakistani leaders who hear President Bush and his envoys calling for nuclear restraint and a return to diplomacy.

The rhetoric from both India and Pakistan on the willingness to use nuclear weapons forced the Bush administration into a high-profile strategy. On the one hand the Pentagon came with the assessment of what would be the first impact of a nuclear showdown in South Asia – at least 12 million casualties initially and a very large number, perhaps seven more million, to be added later. India-Pakistan tensions have become a major factor that complicates the US War on Terror. It is only natural that a sustained effort is made by both the US and the UK to defuse the situation. Senior officials of both countries have made visits to the subcontinent a regular feature of their diplomatic activity.

There are three clear pointers in the Anglo-US agenda. One, sustained pressure on both India and Pakistan to proceed with de-escalation; two, even-handedness in the dealings with New Delhi and Islamabad; and three, accelerated steps to resolve the Kashmir problem. The last is undoubtedly the most significant. The two Western powers will call it 'continued engagement' with India and Pakistan. India will describe it as 'facilitation' while to Pakistan it will be 'mediation' or 'third party role'. At the moment however the main concern of the two Western powers is de-escalation. The idioms currently used by the US and the UK are meant to achieve this objective. 'Infiltration is down across the Line of Control but it needs to be made permanent and further steps need to be taken', was the formulation by Jack Straw, British Foreign Secretary during a visit to India and Pakistan in the third week of July 2002.

Washington is trying to perform a balancing act in dealing with India and Pakistan. Washington's even-handedness, evident of late, was reflected in two pronouncements in the middle of July – rejection of a plebiscite as a way out of the Kashmir tangle, on the one hand, and a refusal to accede to India's plea to declare Pakistan a terrorist state, on the other. On the first, the US Assistant Secretary of State for South Asia, Christina Rocca stated, 'The US supported successive UN efforts. But in 1972, India and Pakistan reached an agreement [Shimla] that it would be a bilateral issue. We support India and Pakistan and we are working towards getting these two countries to the table to resolve this issue'.[8] It thus vindicated New Delhi's position that the Shimla agreement had an over-riding effect on the UN resolutions, adopted more than two decades earlier. The US however rejected India's plea to declare Pakistan a terrorist state. Dealing with the demand by India's Deputy Prime Minister Advani, a State Department spokesman emphasized that 'Pakistan has been a very stalwart ally in the fight against terrorism. President Musharraf has announced some fairly bold measures and our interest is in helping Pakistan'.

It has been a tightrope walk for the Pakistani government with regard to the Iraq crisis in the last several weeks. It has been under enormous pressure from the US on which it is so dependent for economic and defence needs. Pakistan knows it will collapse if the US turns against it and its President has voiced concerns about possible attack from the US. As a member of the Security Council it was directly under the strict scrutiny of the US regarding its positions within that body. At the same time Pakistani government had to reckon with the massive and mounting anti-war movement in the country. Nine days after the war against Iraq started, its Prime Minister Mir Zafarullah Khan Jamali called for a halt to war and announced it was exploring all avenues to send humanitarian relief as soon as possible.

Even after the US started its massive military campaign against Iraq on March 19, 2003, defying the United Nations, international laws and the international community, the Indian government stuck to what it called the 'middle path'. The Vajpayee government had already rejected opposition demands for a resolution by Parliament on the crisis. The Prime Minister and the Foreign Minister scrupulously avoided mentioning the United States in any of the statements made inside or outside the Parliament. In its studied reluctance to condemn the US action the Indian government claimed it was gaining space to defend its long-term interests in Iraq and Gulf. Its misconceived perceptions on security and economic interests were based on the assumption that the US will dominate the West Asia region unchallenged. It was also clear that the preoccupation with Pakistan moulded New Delhi's thinking on terrorism and it did not want the focus to be shifted to any other region.

India, the founder leader of the Non-Aligned Movement, was not even prepared to support the position of the NAM summit held a few weeks before the war, in which Prime Minister Vajpayee had participated. At the Summit, Vajpayee lectured the Iraqi President on the need to disarm, without a word of criticism against those who in violation of the UN Charter were resorting to threat of force to enforce their will. The NAM Summit declaration categorically rejected war as a means to deal with the crisis. During the visit of Ali Akbar Veliyati, the special envoy of Iranian President Mohammed Khatami, on March 23, the Indian government made it clear that it was not willing to take any initiative through NAM or otherwise on Iraq which could jeopardize New Delhi's improved equation with Washington.

It was clear to everybody including Washington that the message of the 'middle path' was that the Indian government was 'not against' the US. This was seen against the background of India's repeated criticism of Iraq's 'non-compliance' with the relevant UN resolutions. By making the fear of alienating the US the operative factor in dealing with perhaps the most critical international issue of our times, India was totally abandoning principles.

It appears that the only prism that the Indian foreign policy establishment uses in looking at the world is 'Kashmir terrorism made in Pakistan'. 'India seems to be drawing a link between American support for its position on Pakistan and Kashmir with its statements on the ongoing military invasion of Iraq', wrote Amit Baruah in *The Hindu* of March 28, 2003. 'India seems to be drawing connections between what the US says on India-Pakistan-Kashmir issues and India's formulation on the Iraqi issue. The message coming from official circles is that India's concerns in the immediate neighbourhood are far more important than simply sticking to principles so far as the war on Iraq is concerned'. In fact this was the message that the Prime Minister had given at the All-Party meeting on March 22: 'We should be careful that neither our internal debate nor our external actions deflect our attention or those of the world, away from the real source of terrorism in our neighbourhood', he said.

It is not known what assistance India gives to the US directly or indirectly. The official position is that no assistance has been requested. It is known that the US uses Indian airspace for the flights of its military aircraft from Diego Garcia to Kuwait. It is also possible that several US naval vessels got 'relief' from their 'duties' in the Indian Ocean and could go to the Gulf region because of the active presence of the Indian Navy. One of Washington's most senior army officers visited New Delhi in the beginning of February 2003 and had discussions with the chiefs of the Indian Army and Navy. The visit by US Army Chief of Staff General Eric Shinseki was the first high-level visit from a senior member of US defence forces since New Delhi and Washington held joint military exercises. Indian officials did not provide any details about the discussions though they hinted that the Kashmir issue topped the agenda. But the visit of General Shinseki six weeks prior to a 'scheduled war' against Iraq naturally raised questions about India's role.

It was not without significance that on March 26, the very day the Security Council was discussing the US attack on Iraq, Chrisitina Rocca, US Assistant Secretary of State for South Asia in her testimony before the Senate Foreign Relations Committee hailed India as a 'rising global power' and said the US was expanding security cooperation with New Delhi through military exchanges and joint exercises. The 'middle path', it was evident, was within the framework of the assigned role for India.

The question may be asked: Is there a middle path between war and peace; between occupation and freedom; between foreign military rule and sovereignty of a nation? The misguided policy makers in New Delhi want us to believe there is. The people of Iraq know better: there is none. It is therefore not surprising that in trying to explain such an untenable and unethical policy, the Indian Prime Minister and the Foreign Minister have to utter inanities bordering on nonsense only to be parroted by spokesmen and emissaries.

The 'middle path' is euphemism for a Washington-approved policy that India, the closest strategic ally of the US in the region, has adopted, when it seeks a prominent regional role in the new imperial world order being fashioned by the US in the name of the War on Terror. The US knows fully well that India is 'with us', i.e., with the Empire and not against it.

As mentioned earlier, one of the direct effects of the War on Terror is the increasing military cooperation between the US and India. The Bush administration's promotion of the Indian government, which is ideologically committed to a militaristic policy, as a 'strategic partner' has added a profoundly destabilizing factor to relations in the Asian region. In May 2002, the US and India held their first joint military exercises in more than four decades in the Indian city of Agra. US embassy spokesman Gordon Duguid said it was 'the largest army exercise ever to take place between US and India and reflected a growing military cooperation. It is taking place in the framework of our ongoing military-to-military relationship and it will be the first of a regular series of exercise'. The American Assistant Secretary of State for South Asia Christina Rocca told a conference organized by the Confederation of Indian Industry that the 'most topical area' of the emerging Indo-US partnership related to military-to-military relations. 'The long-term goal is ambitious and based on strategic, diplomatic and political cooperation as well as sound economic ties. India's and US military forces are now actively developing the capacity to work together effectively'.[9]

The developing US ties with India mark a sharp shift from the relations that prevailed in the subcontinent during the Cold War. India maintained a close economic and strategic relationship with the Soviet Union from where it obtained the bulk of its military hardware. For decades Washington used its alliance with Pakistan and a succession of military juntas there as a counterweight to New Delhi and Moscow in the region. In the 1980s, the CIA used Pakistan as its base to train, fund and arm anti-Communist Mujaheddin groups in Afghanistan. But with the collapse of the Soviet Union in 1991, the whole strategic equation began to shift as Washington sought to establish its domination over the huge oil and gas reserves in former Soviet Central Asia. The Clinton administration imposed sanctions on both Pakistan and India following the series of rival nuclear tests in 1998. But in 1999, Washington exploited clashes between Indian troops and Pakistan-backed Islamic militants in the Kargil region of Kashmir to open up new relations with New Delhi.

Defence and intelligence links developed by Clinton received a further boost under the Bush administration, especially after the September 11 terrorist attacks in the US. The US lifted the remaining sanctions on India over the nuclear tests and accelerated its intelligence sharing with the Indian military establishment, in particular over Islamic extremist groups, including those opposed to Indian rule in Kashmir, whom India considers as 'terrorists'.

The cornerstone of US-Indian military relations is the Defence Policy Group (DPG) formed in 2001 to consolidate previous attempts to coordinate military policies. Joint executive steering groups have also been established between the two countries for each of the three services – army, navy and air force. Like the training exercise in Agra, the DPG has continued to function throughout the current stand-off with Pakistan, even amid the acute tensions that followed the attack on an Indian army base in Kashmir on May 1, 2002.

While New Delhi previously relied on the Soviet Union, and then Russia, for military supplies, US arms sales to India are accelerating rapidly. In April the Indian army acquired eight AN/TPQ-37 Fire-fighters, an artillery-locating radar system, at a cost of $146 million. The Fire-fighter can pinpoint mortar, rocket launchers and artillery at a range of up to 300 km after tracking a shell for just a few seconds.

The US Defence Department underscored the key role of India in US strategic planning, declaring: 'This sale [of the radar system] will contribute to the foreign policy and national security interests of the US by helping to improve the security of a country that has been and continues to be a force for political stability and economic progress in South Asia'. As far as 'stability' and 'progress' are concerned, it should be noted that as the sale took place, around a million Indian and Pakistani troops, backed by artillery, tanks, missiles and warplanes, confronted each other on high alert along the border.

US-Indian military cooperation is not confined to the Indian subcontinent but extends to naval co-operation in a swathe of ocean from the Middle East to South East Asia. In February 2002, the US Navy participated for the first time in an international fleet review organized by the Indian Navy in Mumbai. In December 2001 the two countries reached an agreement on naval cooperation to secure the maritime routes between the Suez Canal and the Malacca Strait. In March, the two navies conducted a combined training exercise in the Malacca Strait. While the joint patrols are taking place under the banner of War on Terror, the real aims are to ensure US control over key naval routes such as the Malacca Strait, through which a substantial portion of world trade, including in oil and gas, passes. Known as 'choke-points', these sea-lanes provide Washington with a means for exerting pressure, direct and indirect, on its rivals in the region.

Yossef Bodansky, the Director of the US Congressional Task Force on Terrorism and Unconventional Warfare, recently pointed to the strategic significance of the Malacca Strait saying: 'The global strategic growth and expansion of aspiring powers can be contained and regulated through the mere control over the movement of their naval forces through the Strait of Malacca'. Bodansky also identified the primary target, declaring, 'for Beijing, this reality is increasingly a vital interest'.

The War on Terror has been used as the pretext to set up US military bases in Central Asia, provide military aid to Nepal, establish close military ties in South East Asia, particularly in the Philippines and strengthen relations with Taiwan, Japan and South Korea. Control over the Malacca Strait is a key element in this strategy of encirclement and the choice of India as a partner in this exercise is not accidental. The ambition of the present government in New Delhi to transform India into a world power and the Indian political establishment's characterization of China 'to be India's central strategic competitor economically, technologically, politically and militarily' are important factors.

The significance of the close military and intelligence collaboration between India and Israel deserves mention in this connection. Israel has become the second largest arms supplier for India, next only to Russia. Israel has provided India with sea-to-sea missile radar and other surveillance systems, border monitoring equipment, night vision devices and the upgrading of India's Soviet-era aircraft. In marked contrast to Washington's vigorous opposition to the supply of Phalcon reconnaissance aircraft from Israel to China, the US has given clearance to the delivery of such planes to India. In the third week of February 2003 an agreement was made for supply of advanced Israeli avionic system for the Indian Air Force's new MG 27 combat aircraft. There are reports of Indo-Israeli plans to collaborate on the development of a ballistic missile defence system based on the Israeli Arrow technologies.

The Jerusalem Post of February 28, 2003 had a detailed analysis of the growing collaboration between India and Israel with the caption 'India and Israel Forge a Solid Strategic Alliance'. The relationship between the two countries, which became very close after the BJP-led government came to power, dramatically grew into a strategic alliance in the context of the War on Terror. What is important is that this strategic alliance is endorsed by the US and forms part of the security regime envisioned by the US for West and South Asia and even beyond for the whole Indian Ocean region. *The Jerusalem Post* analysis quoted *Washington Post* columnist Jim Hoagland who wrote in an article, 'A Test of True Allies' that 'India and Israel are the most vibrant democracies in a vast swathe of countries from North Africa through the Himalayas that should now be seen as a single strategic region. Jerusalem and New Delhi are also end points of the US campaign [against terror]'.

India's Home Minister and Deputy Prime Minister L.K. Advani said in an interview to Fox News on January 9 2002, 'Terrorism insofar as we have seen it on 11th September or 1st October or on 10th December has a common source and that common source has described the US, Israel and India as its three main enemies'. So these three countries had a common cause and could forge a common front against terrorism, Advani implied. There was quick positive response to Advani's statement from Tel Aviv.

Notes

1 *The Times of India*, September 20, 2001.

2 Stephen P. Cohen, 'A Distant Region Takes a Centre Stage', *The Brookings Review*, Summer 2002, no. 3.

3 For the text of Vajpayee's message, see *The Hindu*, January 2, 2002.

4 *The Hindu*, January 4, 2002.

5 Ibid.

6 *The Hindustan Times*, December 30, 2001.

7 *The Times of India*, May 19, 1998.

8 *The New York Times*, July 20, 2002.

9 *The Times of India*, May 14, 2002.

10

Other War Fronts in Asia

When the war against Afghanistan was still only a few months old, the Bush administration moved to open up what was officially called 'the second front' in the war on terrorism – South East Asia. This was preceded by a campaign in the US press with a series of articles describing the region as a 'haven' for the Al Qaeda and other Islamic fundamentalist groups. A number of arrests in Singapore and Malaysia provided more grist to the mill with *Time* writing in early February, 'Terrorists are being uncovered throughout South East Asia with nefarious plans, bombs and intriguing connections'. No evidence was forthcoming for these allegations except reference to police and intelligence reports.

The US targeting of South East Asia provoked criticism in the region. In an article entitled 'Wrong Target', the *Far Eastern Economic Review* reported: 'Many people in the region are now saying that US efforts to combat global terrorism are in danger of doing as much harm as good. The US has been described as clumsy, misguided and falling into longstanding local disputes that have festered for years and pose little international threat'.[1] Lee Poh Peng, professor at University Kebangsaan in Malaysia, told the magazine: 'The US campaign is disproportionate to the evidence of terrorism in South East Asia'. The article continued: 'Lee and some other analysts are mystified by the choice of South East Asia for what Bush calls a "second front" in the fight that the US is leading against terrorism. Some speculate about ulterior motives, suggesting that the US wants to regain a strategic toehold after being evicted from Philippine bases a decade earlier'.

It is not a matter of speculation any more. There is enough evidence that, well before September 11, a debate was underway in the US political establishment over the necessity of a more aggressive intervention in the region. Some of the main arguments were set out in a key report in May 2001 by a task force of academics, corporate executives and officials under the auspices of the Council on Foreign Relations. In its memorandum to President Bush, the taskforce stated: 'This is a timely moment for your administration to focus on a region that too often in the past has fallen off our radar screens, always to our peril'.[2] The report critiqued the lack of a 'clear coherent strategy' in the past, a reference to the Clinton years. Under that administration, Washington seized on the Asian economic crisis that erupted in 1997 to push the IMF's long-held plans for sweeping economic restructuring to open up the region's economies to US investors. At the same time Washington pushed for 'democratic reforms', most notably in Indonesia, as a means of refashioning so-called crony capitalist regimes, to meet the requirements of international capital. While not dropping these economic objectives, the taskforce findings argued for different priorities based first and foremost on a more assertive US military stance in the region. 'American influence in the region has waned as a result of a mix of inattentiveness and imperious hectoring, and the perception if not the reality of a belated and inadequate response to the traumatic 1997–98 financial crisis'.

In the background of these concerns about waning influence in the region is the impact of the US defeat in Vietnam. After the US was compelled to withdraw its military forces from Indochina in the mid-1970s, it lost the use of major bases in the

Philippines – the Subic Bay naval facility and the Clark air base. In 1998, the Indonesian military strongman, Suharto, on whom Washington had relied heavily, particularly after the Vietnam War, was forced to resign. The report was calling for a reversal of these political and strategic setback, particularly in conditions where US interests in the region and beyond have expanded and following the 1997–98 financial crisis, political instability has risen markedly.

> Even putting aside the tragedy of the Vietnam War, it is difficult to acknowledge that such a large area, with nearly 525 million people and a $ 700 billion GNP, that is our fifth largest trading partner, could somehow be an afterthought in US policy. This should not be the case, particularly in a part of the world where the United States has fought three major wars over the past six decades, and where the 1997–98 currency crisis threatened to destabilize the entire world financial system.
>
> Of special note are oil and gas reserves and production levels in Indonesia and Brunei. Indonesia, the only Asian member of the OPEC, accounts for 20 per cent of the world's liquefied natural gas (LNG) exports, and its reserves are still not fully known. New oil and gas fields are being discovered there, in Malaysia, Vietnam and the Philippines.

The report pointed to the region's strategic significance as 'a place of great geopolitical consequence that sits aside some of the world's most critical sea-lanes'. More than $ 1.3 trillion worth merchandise trade passed through the Strait of Malacca and Lombok in 1999 – nearly half of the world's trade – including crucial oil supplies from the Persian Gulf to Japan, South Korea and China. 'As a result, any disruption or dislocation of energy supplies would have an immediate and devastating impact on the economies of East Asia and would have significant secondary effects on the US economy as well'. At the top of its list of proposals to address US interest, the report called for the strengthening of the US military presence. 'The highest American priority should still be assigned to maintaining regional security through the prevention of intra-regional conflict and domination by an outside power or coalition. The administration should preserve a credible military presence and a viable regional training and support infrastructure', it stated.

After September 11, the Bush administration rapidly seized the opportunity to give effect to the proposals drawn up by rightwing think tanks like RAND and the Council on Foreign Relations task force. Under strong pressure from Washington, one national leader after another was compelled to offer support, including the use of staging facilities and military bases and the granting of over flight rights for US forces bound for Afghanistan. It was left to the Heritage Foundation, a think tank with close connections to the Republican Party, to spell out that, as in Afghanistan, the War on Terror would ultimately be pursued in South East Asia with or without the express approval of local governments. Dana Dillon and Paolo Pasicolan, after setting out a list of proposals for strengthening US ties in the region, concluded:

> While the preferred solution is to use local governments and local security forces to attack terrorism at its roots, in order to protect Americans from terrorist acts, Washington must always keep open the option of direct military intervention. Should there be a clear and immediate threat to US citizens or property that local security forces in Southeast Asia cannot handle, Washington must be ready to act.[3]

The decision by the Bush administration to open up a 'second front' in South East Asia, then, was neither accidental nor a response to any serious threat. Under the cover of the war on terror, the US decided to press ahead with long-held plans to re-establish military presence in South East Asia and to aggressively assert US economic and strategic interests.

Richard Fischer jr., director of the Heritage Foundation, wrote two years ago that the US-Philippines alliance must be rebuilt against the backdrop of China's assertiveness in South East Asia: 'The lack of defence cooperation between old allies has created a power vacuum [in Asia] that China has been exploiting'.[4] Subsequently, the US response to September 11 has altered the geopolitical landscape in the region, as it has in many parts of the world, and in many ways it is helping to serve what has been defined as US interests and what several South East Asian governments see as theirs as well.

Consider the case of the Philippines. With more than 1,200 troops deployed at the Philippines camp at Tabiwan by early 2002, there was growing support in Washington for widening the war on terrorism in the name of engaging the Abu Sayyaf group. Some observers believe that a continuous escalation of US military presence in the Philippines to help the government crush Islamic extremists could spark an escalation of the long-standing conflict between the rebels and the Philippine army. The politically powerful US Federation of Philippine American Chamber of Commerce quietly cautioned Washington against any actions that may contribute to a rising tide of US 'neo-colonialism' accusations that may define the new bilateral relationship. In the spring of 2002, the Political and Economic Risk Consultancy (PERC), a Hong Kong-based company, issued an intelligence report. The sensitive political document indicated the associated risks for US troops getting bogged down in a protracted and costly conflict in the region.[5] John Gersham, Asia editor, *Foreign Policy in Focus*, writes:

> Even prior to the tragedy of September 11, there was strong

> interest by the Pentagon to expand its role in the Philippines not in terms of regaining permanent bases, which are too expensive, inflexible and political targets, but in terms of expanding access to Philippine ports and airfields for logistical support as well as increasing the number and scope of training and advising exercises, with an idea of having some contingents of US troops on the ground and or in the waters near the Philippines.[6]

America's strategy is to demonstrate a military commitment to crush any extremist Muslim activity with links to international terrorism or Al Qaeda, and in the process to strengthen their relationship with a key historical ally in East Asia. The strategic geographic location of Philippines has always been a major factor for US policy in the region and historically the Philippines has served as a staging ground for US forces in the Pacific from the Second World War to the Vietnam era.

More recently, the United States Agency for International Development (USAID) committed more than $ 200 million to improve the infrastructure in General Santos City, located in the Mindanao region, with the development of major highways, an international airport and port facilities. The expansion of these infrastructure projects in the southern Philippines benefits commercial interests and efforts to undermine support for insurgents, but also provides for a ready-made strategic South East Asia frontline for the US. Pentagon announced in the third week of February 2003, that about 3,000 troops including 380 Special Forces Green Berets would take part in combat operations aimed at finishing off the Abu Sayyaf group that escaped joint US-Philippines deployment in 2002. That operation was classified as a training mission. The new mission, Pentagon has claimed, will be for combat operations. The Philippines constitution prohibits foreign troops from fighting in the country; unsurprisingly, official spokesmen have stated there would be no combat role for US troops. What is significant is that the strength of the US forces in the Philippines has increased from 1,200 to 4,500 within a very short period, while it is well known that the Abu Sayyaf group numbers not more than 100.

Anticipating the possibility that US military personnel deployed in the Philippines will be accused of human rights abuses, Washington has offered Manila $ 30 million in additional military aid in exchange for an agreement that would exempt US soldiers operating in the Philippines from the International Criminal Court. Senior Washington policy shapers view the present military course as an effective way of rejuvenating the bilateral US-Philippine alliance, strengthening the US military presence in the region, which would be primarily to facilitate US force projection toward China, the South China Sea, the Korean peninsula, the Persian Gulf and Central Asia.

The message of the Council on Foreign Relations Report to Bush was explicit. Drop Clinton's lecturing over democracy, particularly in Indonesia, where the 'preoccupation' with East Timor has led to a Congressional ban on US-Indonesian military ties, and counter Chinese influence in the region, especially in the strategic South China Sea. In relation to Indonesia, the report insisted that, 'The United States must cease hectoring Jakarta and instead do its utmost to help stabilize Indonesian democracy and the Indonesian economy as well as re-engage Indonesia's army'.[7] As US officials lobbied Congress in June 2002 to approve a $ 16 million package of military aid for Indonesia, they were stressing the need to support political stability in the world's largest Muslim nation while downplaying Jakarta's role in the global War on Terror.[8]

Indeed, with regard to Indonesia the American government

has actually modified its position several times regarding the terrorist threat. In its initial response to September 11 the Bush administration pressed Jakarta and other allies to join the war against the Al Qaeda network responsible for the hijack attacks. In the weeks after September 11, US officials warned that Osama bin Laden's Al Qaeda network had infiltrated Indonesia, posing serious danger. 'I think they are more dangerous to Indonesia than they are to the United States', Deputy Secretary of Defence Paul Wolfowitiz, who once served as ambassador to Jakarta, told an Indonesian magazine in 2001 November. Then the Bush administration changed its tune emphasizing Indonesia's stability and not terrorism. One factor in the US decision to stress Indonesian issues was the potential backlash from Indonesian Muslims toward US policy in the Middle East, particularly Washington's 'uncompromising support for Israel', said Meidyatama Suryodiningrat, the managing editor of the *Jakarta Post*. 'The perception remains that Muslims are being victimized' by US policy, Suryodiningrat said. He noted that radical Islamic parties would contest for power in the 2004 national elections in Indonesia. If the economic situation doesn't improve, more young Indonesians could be 'attracted to radical ideologies', he said. 'There is a potential for radical Islamic movements to become popular'.

US military aid and training for Indonesia was suspended in September 1999, in the aftermath of the rampage in East Timor by militias backed by the Indonesian army (TNI). Later that year, Congress adopted the Leaby amendment linking the resumption of military aid to the prosecution of military personnel involved in the atrocities. Since Megawati's visit to Washington soon after the terrorist attacks in America, US-Indonesian military ties have grown closer. There have been security talks at high levels in April. Defence Secretary Rumsfeld visited Jakarta in May and said that a quick resumption of military ties between

Washington and Jakarta would bolster the war against terrorism.

There is strong criticism of US plans to resume military aid to Jakarta. Sidney Jones, the Jakarta representative of the International Crisis Group said it is too far too early to resume direct military aid to the TNI. The $ 16 million package requested by the Bush administration 'sends a very strong signal about the Indonesian TNI involvement with internal security', she said.[9]

The US position regarding terrorist threat in Indonesia changed again, with the bombing of a night club in Bali on October 12, 2002, which claimed almost 200 lives, making it the deadliest terror strike since September 11. Increasing pressure was put on Indonesian authorities to crack down on suspected terrorist groups. The Indonesian Ambassador to the United Nations explained to *Jakarta Post* on December 17, 2002, 'Before Bali our relationship [with the US] was somewhat sensitive as the US thought we were not serious about dealing with terrorism. On the other hand Indonesia was skeptical about the presence of local terrorists and was slow to take any action because of the absence of an anti-terrorism law'. Within a month of the Bali bombings Indonesia issued a tough anti-terrorist law. It arrested a number of suspects in connection with the bombings including the alleged leader of the Jamaah Islamiya extremist group, Abu Baker Ba'asyir. Indonesian officials stated on January 7, 2003, that there was no direct evidence of Al Qaeda involvement in the Bali bombings. In addition to the Indonesian police, Australian and American agencies have been involved in the investigation.

While the US has begun indirectly to aid the Indonesian military, the full restoration of military ties depended on Indonesia demonstrating progress in holding accountable those responsible for past human rights abuses. A recent International Crisis Group paper on Indonesia states: 'Better military training will not alter the fact that there is a fundamental lack of political will on the part of Indonesian national civilian and military authorities to exert control over private armies, punish abusive soldiers, end military corruption or proceed with long-promised reforms'.

In contrast to the sharply critical policy of the US bombing campaign in Kosovo, the People's Republic of China has played a quiet but supportive role of the US campaign in Afghanistan through its close diplomatic relations with Pakistan. In fact China has served as a go-between for the US and Pakistan on certain matters. China's cooperation with the US is particularly impressive since the US still has sanctions on China for transferring missile technology to Pakistan even though the US recently lifted proliferation-related sanctions on Pakistan itself. Finally when the US withdrew from ABM treaty on December 13, Chinese leaders offered tepid critiques mixed with constructive and forward-looking responses. A Foreign Ministry spokesman stated simply, 'China is not in favour of missile defence systems'. China had always maintained that the ABM Treaty was 'a cornerstone of global strategic security'.

Although avoiding conflict on its border is clearly in China's national interest, the recent surge in diplomatic leadership and strategic restraints are primarily due to China's domestic economic imperatives. After 14 years of difficult – often acrimonious – negotiations, China finally acceded to the WTO on December 11, 2001. Joining the WTO is perceived by the Chinese people and the leadership as a defining moment for the nation. Despite the sense of achievement it gives, China realizes that adhering to the rigid trade rules set by the WTO will cause substantial economic dislocation and pain in many economic sectors in China, particularly over the next few years. To avoid their traditional and quite rational fear of 'internal calamity and external chaos' Chinese leaders seek a stable strategic environment. To manage the upcoming economic challenges, China will need access to export markets abroad, increased foreign investment, a moderate military budget and diplomatic support.

US officials have repeated the position that the new intensified American military presence is aimed at preventing terrorism and not intended to counter or contain China. But it is well known that in spite of some cooperation on the issue of terrorism in the region, Washington's policy is shaped by the perception of a 'Chinese threat'.

President Bush's State of the Union address on January 29, 2002, gave clear notice that yet another front of the War on Terror is Northeast Asia.

Immediately after the September 11 attacks, South Korean and US forces went into a state of heightened security alert. North Korea claimed this was 'threatening' and broke off ongoing negations on family reunions. But at the international level, following the September 11 events, North Korea had unilaterally moved to sign two UN anti-terrorism treaties and later expressed willingness to sign an additional five.

It was clear that the Bush administration was using September 11 to renew its campaign against North Korea intensively. It made expansive new allegations about Pyongyang's biological weapons programme without any fresh evidence. The President followed up these remarks by directly implicating North Korea in the new War on Terror due to its development of weapons of mass destruction and weapons proliferation, and then retaining North Korea on the State Department's revised list of nations that support terrorism. And then in the famous 'axis of evil' speech, Bush included North Korea along with such distant states Iran and Iraq, America's main enemies, without rhyme or reason.[10]

It was clear that the US was coming up with new justification for reinforcing its expansive military presence in North Asia rather than dealing with terrorism. The calculated attempt to undermine South Korean President Kim Dae Jung's 'Sunshine Policy' was clear evidence of this. An important factor is the US plans for missile defence. As soon as Bush came to power, senior US officials privately asked Kim Dae Jung to offer a public statement of support for missile defence cooperation in Korea. Kim not only refused but subsequently issued a joint statement with visiting Russian President Vladimir Putin reflecting their shared 'concerns' with the US missile defence plans and their support for the ABM treaty. During Kim's Washington trip in March 2001, President Bush raised serious doubts about the Sunshine Policy underlining the danger of the North Korean threat.

> Since coming into office, the Bush strategy has been three-fold: stymie negotiations between Seoul and Pyongyang, undermine the engagement policy of President Kim while supporting his conservative adversaries, and exacerbate South Korean fears of the North's military threat. The primary objective: build missile defences in and around the Korean peninsula, despite the clear reality that they will never defend Seoul from the North's short-range missiles – located a mere three minutes away.[11]

North Korea's surprise admission in early October 2002 to a secret nuclear weapons programme based on uranium enrichment triggered a cascading breakdown of the 1994 Agreed Framework Structure that had kept North Korea's more advanced plutonium-based nuclear programme in check. The admission caused considerable embarrassment to the US administration. The information was made public only on October 16, five days after the Congress voted to authorize military force against Iraq. The administration had no option except to deny that there was a crisis. The White House did not want to deal with a second crisis. Wade L.Huntley explains,

> The Bush administration's de facto policy of 'hostile neglect' towards Pyongyang has been a fundamental source of the current crisis. Bush officials probably assumed that the aggressive policy to disarm Iraq would also bolster confrontational intimidation of North Korea by implicitly signalling that a charter member of the 'axis of evil' it could become subject to the same type of pressure. But Kim Jong Il seems to have noticed a key point that the Bush team apparently overlooked: as long as the US is preparing for a major war in the Middle East, US threats to resort to the same kind of coercion of North Korea are far less credible. Kim Jong Il's government probably also concluded that only possession of a credible nuclear threat could spare North Korea from Iraq's fate.[12]

Four months before Pyongyang admitted its secret nuclear weapon programme, the CIA had delivered a comprehensive analysis of North Korea's nuclear ambitions to President Bush and his top advisers. The report stated that North Korea had been violating international law – and agreements with South Korea and US – by secretly obtaining the means to produce weapons grade plutonium. However, 'The document's most politically sensitive information however was about Pakistan. Since 1997 the CIA said Pakistan has been sharing sophisticated technology, warhead, design information and weapon-testing data with the Pyongyang regime. Pakistan, one of Bush administration's important allies in the war against terrorism was helping North Korea to build the bomb'.[13]

It is not only a question of dealing with a second crisis that the US faces. The official American policy as outlined in the *National Strategy to Combat Weapons of Mass Destruction* (published in December 2000) authorizes the military 'to detect and destroy an adversary's WMD assets before these weapons are used'. The US is ready to attack Iraq even though it has neither nuclear weapons nor the missile power to hit North America. Yet it claims there is no crisis with regard to North Korea which possesses nuclear weapons and the means to deliver them. This blatant double standard has considerably weakened US case for war against Iraq and shown that it is not the possession or otherwise of WMD that is the issue for the US with regard to Iraq.

On the other hand, though, if there are reasons other than those related to WMD for war against Iraq, there may be reasons other than WMD for not acting against North Korea. All four major players in the region – China, South Korea, Japan and the US – find it convenient to keep North Korea alive, according to Erich Weingartner, an expert on North Korea.[14] South Korea's reasoning is purely practical. If the North Korean regime of Kim Jong Il were to collapse suddenly, the South would be faced with the massive cost of absorbing a famine-struck population almost equal to its own. Given the dismal state of North's economy, reunification of the Korean peninsula would put unbearable strain on the South. China's reasoning is also practical. Historically, Korea has been in China's sphere of influence, a buffer protecting its flank from Japan and the wider world. If North Korea were to collapse, China fears it would be faced with an American ally right up against its border, an ally containing US bases and troops. Better for China to have the certainty of an anti-American regime, no matter how nutty, between it and the reality – or even the possibility – of US troops. Washington's reasons for keeping the North alive stem from a reverse fear, says Weingartner. Without a plausible threat to the region from North Korea, the US would have no justification for its military bases in either South Korea or Japan. Indeed there is already considerable domestic pressure on both the Japanese and South Korean governments to close US bases.

Pyongyang has been demanding direct talks with the US

as the only way to resolve the dispute. Washington says it won't be blackmailed into dialogue and has insisted a resolution is found only through broad-based multilateral diplomacy. Washington's strategy on North Korea will depend on what happens with regard to its Iraq project.

In a security landscape deliberately changed by US policies in the post-September 11 period, Asia is entering a period of intensified arms race. New arms deals and alliances in the making initiated by the US along with upgradation of weapons systems and modernization of forces in the region have pushed the Asian military situation to a qualitatively new plane. Concerns about dangers of nuclear weapons were dramatically heightened during the stand-off between India and Pakistan. North Korea's nuclear weapon programme has made the situation even more serious and complex.

Dmitri Trenin, deputy director of the Carnegie Moscow Centre, referred to the acquisition of nuclear weapons by Asian powers as the advent of a second nuclear age. 'The emergence of nuclear weapons in South Asia leaves a qualitative and new strategic environment for Asia', said Trenin. 'Modernization of Chinese strategic forces adds to this new environment', he said, adding the new situation 'calls for a new level of strategic interaction in Asia and there is a new need for a system of nuclear arms control and nuclear safety'.[15] Luo Renshi, a senior research fellow at the China Institute for International Strategic Studies in Beijing, said any deployment by the US of a missile defence system would force China to develop and deploy its own system.

The region is now close to the classic definition of an arms race where an acquisition of a weapon by one country leads a neighbour to do the same. In a way during the past decade, after the end of the Cold War the Asian region did not witness an arms race worth mentioning. Now all countries big and small across

Asia including China, India, Pakistan, Indonesia, Philippines, Australia, Singapore and Malaysia are in the race strengthening military forces and acquiring new weapons. Steven Metz, director of research and chairman for regional strategy and planning at the US Army Strategic Institute, said Asia's diversity should make the region a 'laboratory for the evolution of military affairs in the coming decade'. The War on Terror has accelerated the process of militarization of Asia.

Asia, from West to North East, is currently the main theatre of America's War on Terror.

Notes

1 *Far Eastern Economic Review*, January 18, 2002.

2 'The US and South East Asia. A Policy Agenda for the New Administration', *Council on Foreign Relations*, May 2001.

3 Dana Dillon and Paolo Pasicolan, 'South East Asia and the War Against Terrorism', *Heritage Foundation*, October 2001.

4 Morites Sison, 'War on Terror Smoothens US Role in Philippines', *IPS*, March 25, 2002.

5 James Borton, 'Philippines Remains a Strategic Archipelago for US' *Asia Times*, June 25, 2002.

6 John Gershman, 'The US Takes Anti-Terror War to the Philippines', *Foreign Policy in Focus*, January 15, 2002.

7 'The US and South East Asia. A Policy Agenda for the New Administration', *Council on Foreign Relations*, May 2001.

8 Tim Shorrock, 'Critics on Warpath against US Military aid to Jakarta', *Asia Times*, June 25, 2002.

9 Ibid.

10 James Reilly, 'The US War on Terror and East Asia', *Foreign Policy in Focus*, Policy Report, February 2002.

11 Ibid.

12 'Coping With North Korea', *Foreign Policy in Focus Policy Report*, February 2003.

13 Seymour M. Hersch, 'The Cold Test', *The New Yorker*, January 27, 2003.

14 Thomas Wilkom, 'Practical Policy on North Korea', *Toronto Star*, February 18, 2003.

15 AFP, Singapore, February 25, 2002.

11

Globalization and the War on Terror

In the immediate aftermath of the September 11 terrorist attacks, President Bush told US citizens that the country faced the 'first war of the twenty-first century'. A few days later Vice President Dick Cheney vowed that the coming conflict would be 'global in scope'. Is the first war of the twenty-first century also the first major war in the age of globalization? Some would say that the war against Serbia in 1999 was the first one. But some would go even further in history. They would say that the first Gulf War was both the first war of the twenty-first century and the first major war in the age of globalization. As mentioned earlier, Eric Hobsbawm in his *The Short Twentieth Century* says that the twenty-first century began in 1991 with the collapse of the Soviet Union. The end of the twentieth century came with the end of the Cold War. The Gulf War was about a 'new world order' of which globalization was to be an important component.

We are now in the age of the War on Terror. We are told this may go on for a long period like the Cold War.

Much has been written about how the forces of globalization – the unremitting expansion of market forces, the lightning speed with which capital movements take place around the globe and the constant effort for realizing greater economic efficiency – influence everything from indigenous cultures and environmental regulation to labour standards and pattern of products. Yet remarkably little attention has been paid to globalization's potential impact on global conflict, and vice versa. Perhaps we have unintentionally subscribed to the persistent optimism of the prophets of globalization who either inferred or emphatically stated that conditions of globalization make a major sustained conflict most unlikely. However, the terrorist attacks, and perhaps more significantly the War on Terror, have altered that comfortable assumption.

Fareed Zakaria gives his explanation of the connection between globalization and terrorism: 'Two factors made the attack of September 11 possible: globalization and human nature. Neither is likely to change. . . . Free trade, the technological revolution, information superhighway, all these wondrous aspects of the open world economy make it easier than ever before to penetrate and disrupt it'.[1] Zakaria, however, makes the link only through the technological aspects of globalization that the terrorists made use of in devising their strategy. *The International Herald Tribune/ PEW* poll suggested that much of the world viewed the attacks on the US as a symptom of increasingly bitter polarization between the 'haves' and the 'have-nots'. Marwan Bishara commented about the 'asymmetric threat from terrorists growing out of the incredible quantitative difference of force and of riches between North and South'. As Robert Wade puts it, 'While the West has been trumpeting the values of globalization, the gap between the rich and the poor has actually been widening'.[2] Some analysts have also pointed out that a defining feature of world politics in the late twentieth century is the decline in the frequency of warfare between industrialized states in the core of the international system. This decline is often accounted for by reference to the extension of a 'zone of peace' among democratic states.

An emphasis on globalization prompts analysis of the international system as a whole and compels recognition of the mutually constituent relations between the so-called zones of war and peace. The role of force in globalization prompts a rethinking of the basic unit of analysis in these debates – the state as a juridically defined, territorially bound and nationally constituted entity drawing attention to the international nature of military and police power in empire and imperial states. According to Tarak Barkawi and Mark Laffey,

> Globalization emerges out of earlier forms of global social changes associated with Western imperialism and the internationalization of capital. The context of the democratic peace then includes not only the advent of a zone of peace among core states but also internationalist relations of domination and subordination in the periphery and the resulting practices of accommodation and resistance.
>
> The merging of industry, technology and bureaucracy into a machinery for waging war contributed directly to the militarization of society. Locating the context of democracy and war in globalization reveals how misleading is any analysis that takes the categories that enable the democratic peace hypothesis as fixed. It leads to recognition of the integral relations between developments in the liberal democratic core and elsewhere and so prompts analysis of the international system not so divided into zones of peace and war but as a structured whole.[3]

Therefore it should not be surprising that the 'zone of war' crashed into the 'zone of peace'.

Examining the role of force in globalization enables a critique of the view of the state as a sovereign territorial entity or 'bordered power container' that informs the democratic peace debates. This critique proceeds along the core dimension of state power – force – and draws attention to the fact that coercive power is not only projected out of a national sovereign territory but is also constituted transnationally. Force is integral to the process of globalization. Colonial and client armies and police force were a central component of the forces available to imperial states both for security and expansion in the non-European world as well as for inter-state competition and total war in Europe.

US hegemony in the new global order has been the subject of much discussion. In the early 1990s, Washington set itself three objectives: to make the global balance resulting from the end of the Cold War, to ensure its ideological lead and military supremacy, and to create an economic environment favourable to its own interests. For the most part these objectives have been achieved. Admittedly international balances are not static and hegemony does not mean absolute freedom of action. But no country or group of countries appears able to constitute a political counter-weight to the US in the foreseeable future. As Thomas Friedman puts it, 'In the globalization system, the US is now the sole and dominant superpower and all other nations are subordinate to it one degree or another'.[4] The same writer wrote an article in the *New York Times*, which carried the illustration of an American flag superimposed on a fist. In this article, Friedman argued that

> for globalism to work, America can't be afraid to act like the almighty superpower it is. The hidden hand of the market will never work without a hidden fist. McDonald s cannot flourish without McDonnel Douglas, the designer of the F-15. And the hidden fist that keeps the world safe for Silicon Valley's technologies is called the United States Army, Air Force and Marine Corps.[5]

As Kevin Danaher, Cofounder of Global Exchange commented, 'It has been said that the invisible hand of the market can't operate without the invisible fist that is military power. The problem is that the market's hand is not invisible for millions of parents whose children are going hungry because of the inequality built into the global economy. And the fist is not invisible for the victims of the so-called "collateral damage"'.[6]

President Clinton himself admitted the relation between American military action and trade, the most important component of globalization. This is what he said about the war against Yugoslavia: 'If we are going to have a strong economic relationship that includes our ability to sell around the world, Europe has got to be the key. That is what the Kosovo thing is all about'.[7] William Cohen, US Defence Secretary at the time, in remarks to reporters prior to his speech at Microsoft Corporation in Seattle, put it this way: 'The prosperity that companies like Microsoft now enjoy could not occur without having the strong military that we have'.[8] It was evident that the attempt was to back up economic globalization by new global security arrangements and the Kosovo conflict provided the first opportunity to sketch in its main components.

The technological gap between the US and the rest of the world is now so great that the two major wars of 1990s, Iraq and Serbia, as well as Afghanistan in 2001 and Iraq now, can be compared to the colonial expeditions of the last quarter of the nineteenth century. A loose working relation now exists among governmental, military, and business interests spanning the computer, media and informational industries. No less than the geostrategists, this group has its eyes focused on an American-directed world and insists that means of achieving this is the electronically based information/media component that confers cultural and general power. 'For the US the central objective of an information age foreign policy must be to win the battle of the world's information flows, dominating the airwaves as Great Britain once ruled the waves of the sea'.[9]

The United Nations has been restructured through the Bretton Woods institutions. The Security Council has become little more than an extension of Western, or rather US, foreign policy, notwithstanding its lack of approval for the American aggression in Iraq in 2003. It is a foreign policy increasingly fashioned to support a 'global governance', the main objective of which is to promote 'dynamic open free markets' for globalization. In June 1997, the President of the UN General Assembly announced that corporations would be given a formal role in UN decision making. Secretary General Kofi Annan suggested that he would like to see more opportunities for companies to set global standards. The UN, which until a few years ago had sought to defend poor countries from big business, would now seek to help big business to overcome the resistance of poor countries.

In July 2000, Annan launched an ambitious partnership, a 'global compact' with fifty of the world's biggest and most controversial corporations. The corporations promised to respect their workers and their environment. Annan told them that the UN would safeguard open markets while at the same time creating a human face for the global economy. The UN, in other words, appears to be turning itself into an enforcement agency for the global economy, helping Western corporations to penetrate new markets while avoiding the regulations, which would be the only effective means of holding them to account. The UN risks becoming a vehicle for the new colonialism of the Third World that rests on free trade and liberalized rules for investment, privatization and deregulation, all backed by the military might of the US. By making peace with power, the UN is declaring war upon the powerless.

What, then, is the relationship between globalization and militarization? Steven Staples comments:

> Globalization and militarism should be seen as two sides of the

> same coin. On one side, globalization promotes the conditions that lead to unrest, inequality, conflict and ultimately war. On the other side, globalization fuels the means to wage war by protecting and promoting the military industries needed to produce sophisticated weaponry. This weaponry is used – or its use is threatened – to protect the investments of transnational corporations and their shareholders.[10]

Globalization promotes inequality, unrest and conflict. Economic inequality is growing: more conflicts and civil wars are emerging. It is important to see a connection between these two situations.

Proponents of global economic integration argue that globalization promotes peace and economic development in the Third World. They assert that 'all boats rise with the tide' when investors and corporations make higher profits. However, there is precious little evidence that this is true and substantial evidence of the opposite.

The United Nation's *Human Development Report 1999* noted that globalization is creating new threats to human security. Economic inequality between Northern and Southern nations has worsened, not improved. There are more wars being fought today – mostly in the Third World – than there were during the Cold War. Most are not wars between countries, but civil wars where the majority of those who die are civilians, not soldiers. The mainstream media frequently oversimplify the causes of war, with claims that they are rooted in religious or ethnic differences. While such differences are made use of in conflicts, a closer examination reveals that the underlying source of most conflicts is economic in nature. Financial instability, economic inequality, competition for resources, and environmental degradation – all root causes of war – are exacerbated by globalization.

The Asian financial crisis of the late 1990s resulted in a terrible human cost. The economies of Thailand, South Korea, and Indonesia crumbled in the crisis. These countries previously held up by neo-liberal economists as the darlings of globalization, were reduced to riots and financial ruin. The International Monetary Fund (IMF) stepped in to rescue foreign investors and impose austerity programmes that opened the way for an invasion by foreign corporations that bought up assets devalued by capital flight and threw millions of people out of work. Political upheaval and conflict ensued, costing thousands of lives. Argentina is the latest example of the high cost of IMF prescriptions.

Weapons, from handguns to fighter jets, are a profitable business. Generous government contracts, huge profit margins, and inevitable cost over-run ensure spectacular dividends for weapons producers. Conflicts burning throughout the world guarantee plenty of buyers. After a post-Cold War decline, global weapon purchases rose in 2000 to $ 800 billion. In the aftermath of the September 11 attacks, arms production and sales worldwide have spiralled, encouraged by national policies and supported by multilateral economic institutions.[11]

The new global regime of the World Trade Organization (WTO) sets enforceable rules for the inter-state system. Within this regime there is a distinct bias with enabling provisions for the promotion of arms industry and trade. While some peace and disarmament groups have raised this issue, it has not become a prominent item in the demands for the reform of WTO.

The *International Herald Tribune* reported on March 20, 2001, from Washington that 'in a twist to the Pentagon's growing efforts to bolster the US defence industry, the air force has devised an ambitious plan to help Boeing, the world's largest producer of commercial jets, sell a version of its latest jumbo military transport planes to civilian cargo carriers'. The plan calls for an unusual array of financial incentives to encourage private carriers to buy the transport plane, the C-17 Globemaster, including guaranteed government transport business, as well as a Pentagon promise to buy back C-17s from companies that go bankrupt. In exchange, the private haulers would be required to make their C-17s available during war and other emergencies. For Boeing, the plan could create a market in large commercial cargo planes potentially worth billions of dollars.

The reason for this 'twist' is that while the US government cannot subsidize commercial jets or civilian cargo carriers, it can subsidize military transport planes. Arms manufacturers are deriving special protection and benefits from the WTO. While the WTO allows countries to challenge each other or itself challenges laws and regulations on labour, environment, human rights and consumer protection as 'non-tariff trade barriers' which limit corporate profits, activities of states in the military sphere are exempt from challenge under WTO rules. A highly significant provision – article XXI of the General Agreement on Trade and Tariff (GATT), the main treaty under which WTO functions – states that a country cannot be prevented from taking any action that 'it considers necessary for the protection of its essential interests . . . relating to the traffic in arms, ammunition, and implements of war and such traffic in other goods and materials as is carried out directly for the purpose of supplying a military establishment [or] taken in time of war or other emergency in international relations'. This security exception is part of the WTO as well as other international trade agreements. It provides a blanket exception of military spending for any reason related to national security, based on the premise that the fundamental role of the government is to provide for a military to protect the country and police force to maintain order within it. Article XXI is the most powerful exception in the WTO because it permits governments to define for themselves their 'essential security interests' that can include anything in research, production and export.

Government subsidies often result in cheaper weapons. For arms-importing countries, the security exception means more bang for the bucks spent buying weapons abroad and a heightened risk of regional conflict escalation. As John Feffe explains:

> Structural adjustment programmes – another key component of globalization – permit a similar security exception to their free market focus. Acting on the advice and pressure of the International Monetary Fund, governments have slashed government budgets and privatized government industries. But defence budgets have largely remained off limits to the dictates of the international financial institutions (IFIs). Although many governments have privatized military production and even some military operations, they maintain indirect subsidies (through tax relief or export guarantees) and have arranged continued access to civilian infrastructure for military purposes.
>
> Globalization in the form of increased world trade and neo-liberal structural adjustment is in theory designed to increase competition. Companies compete against one another on a global basis to produce the cheapest and most profitable products and governments step back from the economy to allow this competition free rein. But the logic of the modern military system is quite different. While macro-policy is conflict driven, US global military dominance is held together by cooperation: building alliances, conducting joint exercises, selling compatible weaponry and supplying spare parts. The majority of weapons sales are part of global alliances – between the US and Israel, the US and South Korea and so on.[12]

Several new alliances are being forged by the US in the context of the War on Terror.

In the name of national security, governments intervene repeatedly in their economies to enhance the competitive edge of their military producers in the international marketplace. State planned economies are fast disappearing in the era of globalization, except for the charmed circle that controls the military-corporate complex. Multilateral economic institutions such as the WTO and the IMF have helped sustain an environment in which this set can flourish. The security exception enables governments to globalize their military production while largely bypassing the fierce competitive forces of globalization. Globalization and transnationalization of defence/military corporations have replaced the military-industrial complex of the Cold War economy with a military-corporate complex of the new global economy. This is based upon the dominance of corporate interests over those of the state. The state has lost even the little say it had in the era of the military-industrial complex.

The US is moving full speed ahead on its missile defence programme with events of September 11 giving a big boost to the scheme. Missile defence or 'Star Wars' advocates maintain that the terrorist attack demonstrated the kind of future assault – the next time around with missiles – the US must seek to offset. US Space Command's Report *Vision for 2020* puts the space programme in terms of furthering corporate-led globalization and maintaining US economic and political dominance by protecting 'US interests and investments' around the globe.

World military spending grew two per cent in 2001, according to official figures, but the increase is much bigger when outlays prompted by the September 11 attacks are included, the Stockholm International Peace Research Institute (SIPRI) said in the 33rd edition of its *Yearbook*. 'But it is an underestimate based on adopted budgets. The increase will be much larger due to September 11, which has led to additional expenditure in the United States but also in other countries'. The Organization for Economic Cooperation and Development (OECD) said in a report on the effects of September 11 that increased military spending reduced economic growth in the longer term. SIPRI Director Daniel Rotfield said combating terrorism had become a high priority for Western governments after September 11. 'However', he pointed out, 'the transatlantic community is confronted with a disagreement over the main aim: whether to focus on disrupting and defeating the Al Qaeda network or eliminating the roots of terrorism with broader range of polices'.[13]

The role of politics and state is the subject of renewed debate after September 11. Fareed Zakaria says,

> The 1990s produced a paradigm through which to view the world: globalization. It held that capitalism, trade and technological revolutions were transforming the world and breaking down old obstacles and mind-sets. Global capitalism was the only game in town, and countries had to play by its rules or be left behind – far behind. Politics would have to accommodate itself to those new realities moving from the centre stage to a supporting role.
>
> Since September 11 we seem to have been looking at the world using a new paradigm. Politics is back, culture is back, ideology is back, and above all government is back. Government is back because it is needed to fulfil its fundamental role: the provision of security for its citizens.[14]

Similar views were expressed by Klaus Schwab, founder-president of the World Economic Forum, in a speech in Mumbai to a meeting of the Confederation of Indian Industries on December 3, 2001. He said that for some time impression had gained ground that economics is more important than politics. But recent events have proved that this is not correct. Politics and nation states again came to the centre-stage. The events of September 11 are a turning point to international economic and political order and to the globalization process itself.[15]

It was soon after the Doha Ministerial Meeting of the WTO that this statement was made by Schwab. He was of course reflecting on the 'politics', which influenced the meeting. In the new political situation created by the war on terror, President Bush's threat that 'if countries are not with the US, they are with the terrorists' had a huge impact on trade negotiations and in particular the outcome of the WTO's Fourth Ministerial Conference. September 11 came at a time when many developing country governments were becoming increasingly critical of the manner in which WTO decisions were made. US reaction to September 11 led to a profound setback to all the plans of resistance they had made. While the launch of a new round of negotiations had been touted as beneficial for developing countries, they knew that nothing could be further from the truth. It was the usual game of the developed countries to gain further control over the resources and economies of the South. September 11 was never discussed in any formal meeting at the WTO. But the US Representative Robert Zoellick, toured the world, meeting with Presidents and Prime Ministers with the message that a new trade round and free trade would stamp out terrorism. His message was taken up promptly by two others: Director General Mike Moore and EU Trade Commissioner Pascal Lany.

The fight to launch a new round of trade talks before Doha was thus shifted away from negotiations primarily carried out in Geneva to talks with heads of governments and trade ministers in the capitals. New trade talks and security matters, only remotely connected earlier, became one and the same issue. For a variety of reasons, many developing countries suddenly found themselves in too vulnerable a situation to continue opposing the USA. The WTO trade agenda of the US and Europe, though starkly self-centred, became a small concession in return for US aid of some sort or the need to be seen actively supporting the new coalition that was being built against terrorism.

The critical question before Doha was whether or not a new round of issues (investment, competition, transparency in government procurement, trade facilitation, further lowering of national tariffs) would be launched. The EU was at the forefront of the campaign, supported by the US. At the end of July 2001, the Director General appeared to be sceptical about a successful launching of the new round. Among the strongest opponents were like-minded group of countries, and in particular India, Pakistan and Malaysia. The impact of the War on Terror on these countries was significant, though in different ways. On Pakistan and India it was direct. The heads of all these states had to agree to support the new round. The Indian Minister of Commerce led a losing battle till the end but his Prime Minister had apparently given an assurance to President Bush during his visit to Washington soon after the September 11 attacks. The War on Terror solved for the WTO an important problem, namely that of launching the new round. The WTO was one of the early victors in the War on Terror.

Long time WTO analyst Chakravarthi Raghavan sarcastically pointed out that the New Round would more accurately be called 'the bin Laden Round'.[16] It is true that many developing countries by virtue of their dependence on the US and EU for markets and preferential trading arrangements, find themselves in a weak position. Nevertheless the room for resistance by the South governments had increased considerably post-Seattle. September 11 eliminated this space and gave the powerful countries a new legitimacy to rule over the economies of the South, in the name of the War on Terror.

The War on Terror aims at making the world safe for globalization.

Notes

1 Fareed Zakaria, 'A Plan for Global Security', *Newsweek* Special Davos Edition, December 2001–February 2002.
2 Both Bishara and Wade have been quoted by Andrew Johnston, 'Disparities in Wealth are seen as Fuel for Terrorism', *International Herald Tribune*, December 19, 2001. See chapter 2 above for the longer quotes.
3 Tarak Barkawi and Mark Laffey, 'The Imperial Peace, Democracy, Force and Globalization', *European Journal of International Relations*, Vol. 5 (4), 1999.
4 Thomas Friedman, *The Lexus and the Olive Tree,* Farren, Strauss and Groux, New York, 1999.
5 *The New York Times*, March 28, 1999.
6 Kevin Danaher, *News Release, Institute for Public Accuracy*, November 9, 2001.
7 Benjamin Schwartz and Christopher Layne, 'The Case Against Intervention in Kosovo', *The Nation*, April 19, 1999.
8 *Associated Press* dispatch, February 18, 1999.
9 David Rathkoff, *Foreign Policy*, September 1997.
10 Steven Staples, *Social Justice Magazine*, Vol. 27, No. 4, 2000.
11 John Feffe, 'Militarization in the Age of Globalization', *Foreign Policy in Focus*, November 5, 2001.
12 Ibid.
13 Martin Walker, 'World Military Spending on Rise after September 11', *Reuters*, June 13, 2002.
14 Fareed Zakaria, 'A Plan for Global Security'.
15 *The Economic Times*, Mumbai, December 4, 2001.
16 Chakravarthi Raghavan, *Third World Network*, 28 October 2001.

12

Reordering the World

In what ways is the War on Terror related to the geo-political aims of the United States and other powers? A clear indication was provided by the British Prime Minister Tony Blair in his address to the Labour Party Conference on October 2, 2001, just four days before the joint US-British attack on Afghanistan began. Blair said that the fight against terrorists should be a 'far wider struggle for a new world order that would uphold human dignity and social justice from the slums of Gaza to the mountain ranges of Afghanistan'. He added that this fight is a battle for values and to protect freedom and justice. 'Let us reorder this world around us'.[1]

Blair's speech was reminiscent of the 'new world order' speech made by President George H. Bush in 1991. Addressing a joint session of the US Congress after the end of the Gulf War, President Bush announced that the allied action, which evicted Iraq from Kuwait had been a war which enabled the United Nations 'to fulfil a historic vision of its founders. Now we can see a new world order coming into view. . . . A world in which freedom and respect for human rights find a home among all nations'.[2]

This, of course, was far from true. It was not any new vision of the international community that inspired the Gulf War, it was America's vested interests. Commenting on a BBC programme on the war, *The Guardian* wrote in January 1996:

> Only five years have passed since the Gulf War. Yet in those five years the public picture of what happened in the west's most demanding military operation has altered dramatically. . . . Perhaps the most important underlying concession in the BBC series is about why the war was actually fought. In reality the Gulf War was fought about oil, as General Brent Scowcraft admitted in the first programme.[3]

General Scowcraft was the National Security Adviser to President Bush. It was not a world order in accordance with the Charter of the United Nations that the US envisioned, but a world order of US hegemony maintained by its military might. It was clear already at that time that the same military power would become the security arrangement for globalization.

Tony Blair expounded his ideas on the new world order in 1999 on the occasion of his visit to America to celebrate the fiftieth anniversary of the NATO alliance. It was in his speech to the Chicago Economic Club that he spoke on his new 'Doctrine of the International Community'.[4] Blair placed NATO's war against Serbia in the context of the profound economic changes that had taken place over the last 20 years. Globalization had 'changed the world in a more fundamental way', he said. 'Globalization is not just an economic, but also a political and security phenomenon', he clarified. The dependence of national economies on the performance of world stock markets means that 'We are witnessing the beginnings of a new doctrine of international community'. Blair explicitly linked the question of financial interdependence with the military policy to be pursued by the major imperialist powers. The obverse side of demanding the establishment of a new economic order based on globalization was that the 'principles of international community' must 'apply to international security'. Speaking about the threat from 'dangerous and ruthless men' like

Saddam Hussein and Slobadan Milosevic, Blair called for NATO to impose order on the world under the auspices of the US – 'by far the strongest state'. This new version of the *Pax Americana* meant that 'non-interference long considered an important principle of international order . . . must be qualified'. At that time also he spoke of values: 'liberty', 'freedom' and 'democracy'. 'The spread of our values makes us safer', Blair said.

It was significant that Blair linked the war against Serbia to economic changes of the previous two decades, in other words, to globalization. US-led NATO intervention in Kosovo and its subsequent bombing of Yugoslavia was trumpeted as a humanitarian effort to halt 'ethnic cleansing'. But Anthony Lake, Director of the Central Intelligence Agency during the Clinton administration, pointed out another dimension: 'Our interventions in Bosnia and Kosovo were not only humanitarian. They were essential to the pursuit of our vision of an undivided Europe. Our vision includes not only integration to the east but also the embrace of southeastern Europe, including the Balkans. And Serbia must be included because it is the region's geographic, economic and diplomatic heart'.[5]

The US considered the strategic location of the Balkans which have the richest mineral resources in all of Europe west of Russia. The US-led NATO onslaught on Serbia was also about oil. It was related to the drive to extend and protect the investments of the transnational corporations (TNCs), especially the oil corporations in the Caspian Sea region. President Clinton's frank, though somewhat blunt, admission may be recalled here: 'If we are going to have a strong economic relationship that includes our ability to sell around the world, Europe has got to be the key. That is what the Kosovo thing is all about'.[6] One may add that precisely this, the 'ability to sell around the world', is what the 'Afghanistan thing', as well as the more recent 'Iraq thing', is all about.

Fossil fuels are the lifeblood of globalization. Oil and gas are the backbone of capital-intensive industrial production as they are the energy source for transportation, for industry and for mechanized agriculture. Oil corporations, which control the extraction, transportation, refinement and distribution of fossil fuel, had a global reach long before the new stage of globalization. They play a vital and crucial role in globalization today. Just as the Gulf War was about oil, the new conflict in South and Central Asia is no less about access to the region's abundant petroleum resources. US influence and military presence in Afghanistan and the Central Asian states, not unlike that over the oil rich Gulf States, would be a major strategic gain according to V.R. Raghavan, a strategic analyst and former general in the Indian army. Raghavan believes that the prospect of a western military presence in a region extending from Turkey to Tajikstan could not have escaped strategists who decided on a military campaign to change the political order of Afghanistan. While the 'Great Game' in Afghanistan was once about czars and commissars seeking access to warm water parts of the Persian Gulf, today it is about laying pipelines to the untapped petroleum reserves of Central Asia. The plans of US oil corporations for the region under the protection of the US have the potential of reconfiguring substantially the energy scenario of the twenty-first century.[7]

A host of writings have appeared attempting to give content and meaning to the new world order in the context of the War on Terror. In general they argue a case for a new colonialism and imperialism by military means and, if needed, by conquest. The close links between globalization and imperialism are affirmed not only by critics but also by ardent supporters of globalization. Oxford Professor Niall Ferguson put the matter bluntly:

> We have to understand what the alternative to failure is. We

> have to call it by its real name. Political globalization is a fancy word for imperialism, imposing our values and institutions on others. However you may dress up, whatever rhetoric you may use, it is not very different in practice to what Great Britain did in the eighteenth and nineteenth centuries. We already have precedents: the new imperialism is already in operation in Bosnia, Kosovo, and East Timor. Essentially it is the imperialism that evolved in the 1920s when League of Nations mandates were the polite word for what were post-Versailles treaty colonies. . . . The future of Afghanistan must, if the war is successfully persecuted, be very similar indeed to those states currently under this kind of international colonial rule. Nothing else will do. Contrary to popular arguments made in the 1960s, imperialism is affordable for the richest economy in the world. The US has the resources, but does it have the guts to act as a global hegemony and make the world a more stable place?[8]

The title of an article by the British historian Paul Johnson in the *Wall Street Journal* is telling: 'The Answer to Terrorism? Colonialism'.[9] Johnson writes: 'America has no alternative but to wage war against states that habitually aid terrorists. President Bush warns the war may be long but he has not, perhaps, yet grasped that America may have to accept long-term political obligations too'. Johnson then asks America and her allies not just to occupy with troops but administer obdurate terrorist states. 'These may eventually include not only Afghanistan but Iraq, Sudan, Libya, Iran and Syria. Democratic regimes willing to abide by international law will be implanted where possible, but a Western presence seems unavoidable in some cases'. Johnson is gracious enough to give a UN cover to this colonization. 'It should not be difficult to devise a new form of United Nations mandate that places terrorist states under responsible supervision'. Johnson theorizes that the war against terrorism will lead to a new form of colonialism – of the benign or respectable kind – by the 'great civilized powers'.

If Johnson addressed President Bush, just a day later *Financial Times* columnist Martin Wolf addressed British Prime Minister Tony Blair.[10] 'Mr Blair views today's events as a chance to reorder the world. Yet even he may not realize how radical that reordering must be'. Wolf based his call for a 'new imperialism' on the concept of the so-called 'failed state' of which Afghanistan is but an extreme example. Wolf cited the work of British diplomat Robert Cooper – foreign policy adviser to Tony Blair – who pointed to the emergence of a 'zone of chaos', including Afghanistan. Such areas were not new, Cooper wrote, but were previously isolated from the rest of the world. 'Not so today. . . . If they become too dangerous for the established states to tolerate, it is possible to imagine a defensive imperialism'.

The argument that 'failed states' provide the justification for imperialist rule is specious and hypocritical. The so-called 'failed state' is most often a direct product of the intervention of imperialist powers – organizing coups, stoking up civil wars and ethnic conflicts for their own purposes, and arming repressive regimes – and the imposition of economic polices under globalization creating social disaster for the people of these countries. The proponents of 'new imperialism' conveniently forget to examine how the Taliban got to the top of 'failed' Afghanistan in the first place. The Taliban are eminently an Afghan, Pashtun and tribal movement. It is easy to forget that they are a direct product of the Saudi-American financed anti-USSR jihad of the 1980s. When they took power in Kabul in 1996 they had the blessings of the US.

Afghanistan was beyond 'failed' as a state in 1996. But at that

> time the Taliban were regarded as a convenient tool for the implementation of another classic American business plan: the construction of oil and gas pipelines from the Central Asian republics through Afghanistan, with Karachi as a major destination. The Taliban would theoretically control the whole country, impose law and order, and guarantee a safe trading environment.[11]

Because of the considerable influence they have on British foreign policy, Robert Cooper's views on 'new imperialism' need a closer look. His call for a 'new imperialism' came in a publication of the Foreign Policy Centre in March 2002, with a foreword by Prime Minister Blair.[12] Cooper first advertised his new-colonialist agenda back in 1996, in his book *The Post-Modern State and the World Order*. His subsequent essay, published as part of a compilation in 'Reordering the World – the long-term implications of 11 September', is largely a heavily edited version of his first, but with a different conclusion. In both, Cooper argues that the Western powers had been too quick to proclaim the establishment of a 'new world order' in 1991, following the collapse of the Soviet Union and Eastern bloc regimes, and the subsequent war in the Gulf. According to him this is the time for the re-ordering of the world by imperialist intervention. Not the old-fashioned imperialism which was driven by territorial interests and which is so unpopular, Cooper soothes, but a 'new imperialism' – one that arises 'from defensive' motives or 'in pursuit of an idea'.

Cooper's views have proved immensely popular and influential within the British Labour establishment. Let us return to Blair's speech to the Labour Party Conference in October 2001, where he called for the US-initiated 'war against terrorism' to become the starting point for the reorganization of the entire world. Referring to the September 11 terror attacks, he asserted,

'This is the moment to seize. The kaleidoscope had been shaken. The pieces are in flux. Soon they will settle again. Before they do, let us re-order the world around us'.[13] Later that month Foreign Secretary Jack Straw gave a speech before the International Institute of Strategic Studies, which borrowed heavily from Cooper. Warning that global stability was threatened by 'distant and misgoverned parts of the world' and 'failed states', countries like Britain had a duty to create 'order out of chaos'. Cooper's 'new imperialism' has become the official ideological underpinning of British foreign policy.

Another call to 'colonize wayward nations' with the application of a 'dose of US imperialism' was made by Max Boot, the opinion page editor of *Wall Street Journal*.[14] Boot took issue with suggestions that the September 11 attack was some kind of 'payback for US imperialism'. 'In fact' Boot countered, 'this analysis is exactly backward: the September 11 attack was the result of insufficient American involvement and ambition. The solution is to be more expansive in the US's goals and more assertive in their implementation'. 'Afghanistan and other troubled lands' – he specifically mentions Iraq – 'today cry out for the sort of enlightened foreign administration once provided by confident Englishmen in jodhpurs and pith helmets'. Boot also is generous enough to give a UN address for imperial conquest.

These writings assume significance against the background of the present US strategy of having long-term military presence in several regions of the world where hitherto there was no such presence. The first Gulf War led to permanent US military presence in the region. The war on Kosovo led to establishment of bases there. The same thing is happening now in Central, South Asia and South East Asia. North Asia already has a heavy military presence. As we have seen there are strategic as well as economic considerations for this military presence.

This has added a new dimension to globalization, which has to be understood as a new form of colonization. Rather than the colonization of territories and peoples as in the past, it is a colonization of the regulators of territories and peoples, that is, nation states. But from Kosovo onwards, we have to concede there is a territorial dimension added to globalization. Some territories have to be under the control and if necessary under the occupation of the US military, for security arrangement in the new stage of globalization. This is a development which needs careful analysis. Globalization buttressed by military might of the US is an important part of the architecture of the new global order. Tony Blair is right: 'The war against terrorists is a wider war for a new world order'.

In his speech to graduating cadets at West Point in June 2002, President Bush declared, 'America has no empire to extend or utopia to establish'. When he spoke to veterans assembled at White House in November, he said America has no territorial ambitions. We don't seek an empire. Our nation is committed to freedom for ourselves and for others'. In this, as in much else, President Bush is wrong. To the US, the new world order is an American empire. We are no longer talking about imperialism in the abstract or merely as an ideology. What we are witnessing is the building of an American empire militarily and territorially. For a long time the concept of imperialism was considered outside the acceptable range of Western political discourse. It is suddenly no longer true. Comparison of the US to imperial Rome and imperial Britain are common within the mainstream press. Terms like 'sole superpower', 'hyperpower', 'hegemon' no longer adequately reflect what the US is and what it is doing. In his seminal essay on America's emerging empire Michael Igantieff wrote:

> Ever since George Washington warned his countrymen against

> foreign entanglements, empire abroad has been seen as the republic's permanent temptation and its political nemesis. Yet what word but 'empire' describes the awesome thing that America is becoming? It is the only nation that polices the world through five global military commands, maintains more than a million men and women at arms in four continents, deploys carrier battle groups on watch in every ocean, guarantees the survival of countries from Israel to South Korea, drives the wheels of global trade and commerce, and fills the hearts and minds of the entire planet with its dreams and desires.[15]

The plan for invading Iraq is part of the empire-building project. As Norman Mailer puts it:

> There is a subtext to what the Bushies are doing as they prepare for war in Iraq. My hypothesis is that President George Bush and many other conservatives have come to the conclusion that the only way they can save America and get it off its present downslope is to become a regime with a greater military presence and drive toward empire. My fear is that Americans might lose their democracy in the process.[16]

Recent changes in the security policy as well as the military doctrine of the US therefore deserve close examination.

Changes in the security policy notably include

- A renewed focus on the role of states in supporting terrorism.
- A shift in emphasis away from stability operations and toward traditional war-fighting missions, and a new emphasis on 'regime removal' as an antidote to 'rogue behaviour'.
- A shift in geographic emphasis toward Asia generally, and within this, a dramatic expansion of military presence and

engagement in Central and South Asia.

- A reorientation of America's presence in Europe; although US forces will remain in Europe in large numbers, these will serve a mainly political function there – substantiating US leadership of NATO – while being made more available for actual operational use outside Europe.
- With regard to alliance policy, an increased willingness to undertake military operations on a unilateral basis and increased reliance on short-term, ad hoc, 'tactical' coalitions and partnerships.
- A broader and more flexible practice of military assistance to other states.
- A substantially increased pace of US military modernization.[17]

On September 20, 2001, the Bush administration released the 2001 *Quadrennial Defence Review*. Mandated by Congress, these four-year reviews are supposed to specify US military strategy and show how it relates to budgets and plans regarding force posture, modernization, readiness, personnel and infrastructure. While generally following earlier *Reviews*, the document did signal a critical shift in US defence strategy and policy with implications for the War on Terror. As Carl Conetta explains,

> One critical difference is that the new *QDR* puts a distinctive emphasis on war-fighting and war-fighting capabilities – much as was the case during the Reagan and first Bush administration. With regard to America's wars it goes further, bringing maximum war objectives to the fore. Beyond seeking decisive victory, it aims for the decisive defeat of adversaries. This it defines ambitiously in terms of 'changing the regime of an adversary state' and 'occupying foreign territory until US strategic objectives are met.[18]

'Changing the regime of an adversary state' and 'occupying foreign territory' are important parts of the Bush doctrine and have serious implications for the War on Terror. They also have to be seen in the context of the relation between war and globalization. As pointed out earlier, the new territorial dimension of globalization requires military control and even occupation by US forces. To quote from the *QDR*, 'At the direction of the President, US forces will be capable of decisively defeating an adversary in the theatres in which US forces are conducting major combat operations by imposing America's will and removing any future threat it could pose. This capability will include the ability to *occupy territory* or set the conditions for *a regime change* if so directed' (emphasis added). Also significant is what the new *QDR* does not say in defining the purposes of US military power. In the 1997 *QDR* the 'respond' imperative included being able to conduct a variety of smaller-scale contingency operations and 'operations other than war'. Unlike the 1997 document, *QDR* 2001 makes no reference at all to peacekeeping, peace-enforcement, and the enforcement of sanctions, preventive deployments, disaster relief or humanitarian operations. This does not mean that the armed forces will desist from all these activities and functions. But it does mean that their role in US thinking and planning has been significantly diminished. The emphasis is mainly if not solely on war fighting for decisive victory.[19]

America's rather open-ended and imaginative process of defining military threats and requirements faced and failed its severest test on September 11. The US was utterly unprepared for the attacks despite eight years of strategic warning and eight months of more immediate warnings. In the months prior to the attack the US had been preoccupied instead with discussions of catastrophic bio-terrorism and the missile threat from 'rogue states'.

After September 11, US security concerns have tended to

sprawl in two directions: first, geographically, and second, functionally or across the threat spectrum.

In the geographic dimension the new *QDR* makes a clear break with the Cold War focus in western Europe and North East Asia. In part this means seeking additional bases and stations beyond these areas and redistributing some assets worldwide to reflect new regional military goals. But a retreat from Europe is not contemplated. US forces will remain there in numbers close to 100,000. Politically this will serve to anchor US leadership of NATO. What will change is the operational role of America's forces in Europe: they will orient more towards contingencies outside the West. Thus, western Europe will come to serve more than before as forward bases for US activities farther east and south. Actually this process has been underway since 1990: planning for two major regional contingencies has focused for a decade on North East Asia and the Gulf – not western Europe – while the US became substantially engaged in the Balkans as well.

> The areas of increased future emphasis will be Central, South and East Asia. China is the target of concern and preparations will likely focus on China-Taiwan conflict scenarios and South China Sea maritime competition. Functionally there will be greater emphasis than before on counter-terrorism, missile defence and homeland protection. But the new *QDR* gives no indication of a corresponding reduction in preparations for a conventional war-fighting scenarios – indeed, it expands their scope. To manage this daunting roster of geographic and functional requirements the Bush administration proposes to combine and utilize the totality of US assets in a new way, applying what it calls a 'new concept of deterrence'.
>
> The new concept of US war-fighting and deterrence emphasizes the strategic and operational effects that the United

> States can impose on its adversaries and prospective competitors. Practically it rests on a foundation of global and rapidly deployable reconnaissance, attack and defence capabilities. On the offensive side these capabilities are geared to attack or threaten from a distance a competitor's military and other vital national assets throughout the depth of the competitor's territory. On the defensive side they aim to shield US and other assets from all manner of attack both locally and globally.[20]

The classified *Nuclear Posture Review* of the US, details of which appeared in the media in the second week of March 2002, revealing Pentagon's ambitious nuclear battle plans, redefines the role of nuclear weapons as fundamental to US defence policy, places new emphasis on the utility of nuclear weapons in US military doctrine and strategy and changes the very concept of deterrence. For the first time, the US is sending strong signals that it is considering new uses of nuclear weapons. 'First use' and 'first strike' are writ large on the nuclear agenda of the US.

The *Review* outlines a number of targets where nuclear weapons might be used. It lists seven countries – China, Russia, Iraq, North Korea, Iran, Libya and Syria – as potential nuclear targets. The review indicates that nuclear weapons could be used under three different types of situations: against targets able to withstand non-nuclear attack; in retaliation for attack with nuclear, biological or chemical weapons, or 'in the event of surprising military developments'. The Pentagon must also draw up plans to use nuclear weapons during an Arab-Israeli conflict, an Iraqi attack on Israel or its neighbours, a North Korean attack on South Korea or a military confrontation between China and Taiwan (a scenario in which Chinese leaders may try forcefully to integrate Taiwan with mainland China). The *Review* further envisages the involvement of countries such as Iran, Syrian and Libya in immediate, potential or unexpected contingencies requiring 'nuclear strike capabilities' against them. It states that the US should be prepared to launch a nuclear strike to destroy stocks of weapons of mass destruction, such as biological and chemical arms.

For more than half a century, the sole use for American nuclear weapons has been to deter a nuclear attack. All that has now changed. The *Review* describes a plan to develop a new class of small nuclear weapons for a nuclear strike force, even while calling for deep cuts in strategic weapons. Instead of limiting nuclear weapons to deterrence, new uses are being sought. The readiness of the US to use nuclear weapons 'in the event of surprising military developments' is ominous in the context of the War on Terror, with its changing and expanding aims and targets. In an editorial, 'America as Nuclear Rogue', the *New York Times* wrote:

> If another country were planning to develop new nuclear weapons and contemplating pre-emptive strikes against a list of non-nuclear powers, Washington would rightly label that nation a dangerous rogue state. Yet such is the course recommended to President Bush by a new Pentagon planning paper.
>
> In a world where numerous countries are developing nuclear, biological and chemical weapons, it is quite right that America retain a credible nuclear deterrent. Where the Pentagon review goes very wrong is in lowering the threshold for using nuclear weapons and in undermining the effectiveness of the Nuclear Non-proliferation Treaty. The treaty, long America's main tool for discouraging non-nuclear weapons from developing nuclear weapons is backed by promises that as long as signatories stay non-nuclear and avoid combat alongside a nuclear ally, they will not be attacked with nuclear weapons. If the Pentagon proposals become American policy, that promise would be

> withdrawn and countries could conclude that they have no motive to stay non-nuclear. In fact they may well decide, they need nuclear weapons to avoid nuclear attack.
>
> Nuclear weapons are not just another part of the military arsenal. They are different, and lowering the threshold for their use is reckless folly.[21]

At one stroke the review changes the concept of deterrence and blurs the distinction between nuclear and conventional weapons. In the words of Deputy Defence Secretary Paul D. Wolfowitz, 'We are looking at a transformation of our deterrence posture from an almost exclusive emphasis on offensive nuclear forces, to a force that includes conventional strike capabilities as well as nuclear strike capabilities'.

The changes in doctrine are related to nuclear weapons and deterrence as well as 'strike-first' and 'hot-pre-emption'. The document *The National Security Strategy of the USA* was presented to the Congress on September 20, 2002. The 33-page document presents the most aggressive approach to national security since the end of the Cold War. It includes the discounting of most non-proliferation treaties in favour of a doctrine of 'counter-proliferation', a reference to everything from missile defence to forcibly dismantling weapons or their components. It declares that the strategies of containment and deterrence – staples of American policy since the 1940s – are all but dead. 'America is now threatened less by conquering states than we are by failing ones' the document states, sounding what amounts to a death knell for many of the key strategies of the Cold War. One of the most striking elements of the new strategy outlined is its insistence that 'the President has no intention of allowing any foreign power to catch up with the huge lead the United States has opened since the fall of the Soviet Union more than a decade ago'. The document argues that while the US will seek allies in the battle against terrorism, 'We will not hesitate to act alone, if necessary, to exercise our right of self-defence by acting pre-emptively'. That includes 'convincing or compelling states to accept their sovereign responsibilities not to aid terrorists'. 'Legal scholars and international jurists often conditioned the legitimacy of pre-emption on the existence of an imminent threat – most often a visible mobilization of armies, navies and air forces preparing to attack. We must *adapt* the concept of imminent threat to the capabilities and objectives of today's adversaries', the document states.

This is the most innovative part of the new strategy. It adopts the doctrine of pre-emptive action – while warning others not to use pre-emption as a pretext for aggression. It makes no mention of the UN in this context, and presumes that the US is the sole judge of legitimacy of its own or any one else's pre-emptive strikes. In sum and in context, the doctrine amounts to a doctrine of global domination. Yet the new strategy is basically flawed. As Charles Knight pointed out,

> You cannot *adapt* the concept of imminent threat. It is something that has clear definition and real meaning. What is going on here is the administration announcing a policy of 'preventive war' without using the term. Instead they are trying to stretch the meaning of pre-emptive action to such an extent it renders meaningless the distinction between pre-emptive and preventive. By invoking the views of legal scholars and international jurists regarding pre-emption they try to cover the fact that preventive war is considered illegal by most such scholars and jurists.[22]

As mentioned earlier, Bush hinted at the new doctrine in his State of the Union address in January 2002, when he labelled

Iraq, Iran and North Korea as an 'axis of evil' and warned that he would not allow them to threaten the US with weapons of mass destruction. The President articulated the doctrine for the first time on June 1, 2002, in his commencement address at West Point.

The new strategy departs significantly from the one published by President Clinton at the end of 1999. While Clinton's strategy relied heavily on enforcing or amending a series of international treaties, from the 1972 Antiballistic Missile Treaty to the Comprehensive Nuclear Test Ban Treaty to Kyoto protocols on the environment, Bush's strategy virtually dismisses all of them. In fact, the new document celebrates his decision to abandon the ABM treaty because it impeded American efforts to build a missile defence system.

A key concept of the Bush doctrine is the notion of international impunity. Military strategists know full well that imperial conquest and occupation invariably involve crimes against civilians. Washington's total definitive rejection of the jurisdiction of the International War Crimes Tribunal over its imperial armies is in essence a licence for crimes against humanity. The *National Security Strategy* document says, 'The US will never subject its citizens to the newly created International Criminal Court – whose jurisdiction does not extend to the Americans'.

Another document titled *National Strategy to Combat Weapons of Mass Destruction* published in December 2002 said, 'An effective strategy for combating Weapons of Mass Destruction (WMD), including their use and proliferation is an integral component of the National Security Strategy of the USA'. It explains how the doctrine of pre-emption applies to WMD. 'Because deterrence may not succeed and because of the potentially devastating consequences of WMD use against our forces and civilian population, US military forces and appropriate civilian agencies must have the capacity to defend against WMD-armed adversaries including in appropriate cases through pre-emptive measures. This requires capabilities to detect and destroy an adversary's WMD assets before these weapons are used'.

What is especially significant about the document is that is was released *after* the UN Security Council had unanimously adopted Resolution 1441 (November 8) and the UN inspections of weapons of mass destruction in Iraq had begun (November 18). By claiming the right in mid-December to defend itself against weapons of mass destruction 'in appropriate cases through pre-emptive measures' and to detect and destroy such weapons before they are used against the US, the US was declaring that irrespective of the process of UN inspections and its results, it would take action against Iraq which it believed had weapons of mass destruction. This in effect made all subsequent discussions on weapons inspection a farce.

NATO has developed its own 'strategic concept' for dealing with future threats, including international terrorism, but the language does not mention pre-emptive action. When asked if he could support such a change in strategy, Lord Robertson, the NATO Secretary-General said that the alliance was a defensive organization, adding, 'We do not go looking for problems to solve'. US Defence Secretary Donald Rumsfeld countered by saying that it was difficult to distinguish between offensive and defensive. A military doctrine that makes no distinction between offensive and defensive is dangerous and a constant threat to peace and stability.

Some defence analysts said that pre-emption carried the risk of causing a crisis to escalate quickly by increasing pressure on both sides to act sooner rather than later – forcing them in the parlance of the nuclear chess game to 'use it or lose it'.

But it is not just pre-emption that we are hearing about

now. The new phrase for geo-strategists in Washington is 'hot pre-emption'. Coined in a speech by former Secretary of State George Shultz, the phrase has been accepted as a further refinement of the so-called Bush doctrine. 'This is war', Shultz told an audience of diplomats at the State Department Foreign Service. 'States must be accountable. We are calling on states to step up their internal responsibilities to end any terrorist presence, while saying that we also reserve, within the framework of our right to self-defence, the right to pre-empt terrorist threats within a state's borders. Not just hot pursuit but hot pre-emption'.[23]

The new doctrines and strategies show how US policy has moved from isolationism to Cold War containment to a mad rush by the US to become an overt military empire.

The international order laid down in 1945 at the end of the Second World War has come to an end. The War on Terror is reordering the world.

Notes

1 *The Guardian*, October 3, 2001.
2 *The New York Times*, March 7, 2001.
3 *The Guardian Weekly*, January 21, 1996.
4 This speech is available online at www.wsws.org.articles/1999/apr1999/blair-a29-shtml.
5 Anthony Lake, *New York Times*, October 6, 2000.
6 Benjamin Schwartz and Christopher Layne, 'The Case against Intervention in Kosovo', *The Nation*, April 19, 1999.
7 *Asia Times*, October 6, 2001.
8 *The Guardian*, October 31, 2001.
9 Paul Johnson, 'The Answer to Terrorism? Colonialism', *The Wall Street Journal*, October 9, 2001.
10 Martin Wolf, 'The Need for a New Imperialism', *Financial Times*, October 10, 2001.
11 Pepe Escobar, 'The New Imperialism', *Asia Times*, November 6, 2001.
12 Robert Cooper, 'Reordering the World: the long term implications of September 11', *Foreign Policy Centre*, London, March 2002.
13 *The Guardian*, October 3, 2001.

14 Boot's article appeared in *The Australian*, October 15, 2001.

15 Michael Ignatieff, 'The American Empire: The Burden', *New York Times Magazine*, January 5, 2003.

16 Norman Mailer, 'Gaining an Empire, Losing Democracy', *International Herald Tribune*, February 25, 2003.

17 Carl Conetta, 'The Pentagon, New Budget, New Strategy and New War', *Project on Defence Alternatives, Briefing Report*, June 25, 2002.

18 Ibid.

19 *Quadrennial Defence Review*, 2001, Pentagon.

20 Carl Conetta, 'The Pentagon, New Budget, New Strategy and New War'.

21 *The New York Times*, March 12, 2002.

22 Charles Knight, 'Essential Elements Missing in the National Security Strategy of 2002', *PDA Commentary*, October 9, 2002.

23 *Asia Times*, June 5, 2001.

Index